JOSEPH SMITH, JR.
PROPHET
BORN SHARON, VERMONT
DECEMBER 23, 1805
DIED CARTHAGE, ILLINOIS
JUNE 27, 1844

❺

❻

1830-1839

1830, April 6: Formally organizes the restored Church of Jesus Christ in Fayette, New York, at the home of Peter Whitmer Sr. (24 years old)

1830, June: Begins the inspired translation of the Bible.

1831, April 30: Becomes the father of twins; both die within three hours of birth.

1831, May 9: Adopts infant twins (Joseph and Julia) from John Murdock, whose wife has recently passed away.

1831, August 3: Dedicates the site for the temple in Independence, Missouri. (25 years old)

1832, February 16: Visions of the Father and Son, premortal events, and three degrees of postresurrection glory.

1832, March 24: Tarred and feathered by a mob in Hiram, Ohio. Beaten, scratched, had hair torn out, and had tooth broken in attempted poisoning. Preaches the next day with enemies in the audience.

1832, March 29: Adopted son (Joseph Murdock) dies from exposure suffered during the mob action of March 24.

1832, November 6: Son Joseph Smith III born.

1833, January 22–23: Organizes the School of the Prophets in Kirtland, Ohio.

1833, July 2: Completes the first draft of the inspired translation of the Bible.

1834, May–June: Leads the Zion's Camp expedition to redeem property taken by mob in Jackson County, Missouri. (28 years old)

1836, March 27: Dedicates the Kirtland Temple. (30 years old)

1836, June 20: Son Frederick G. W. Smith born.

1837, June 4: Informs Heber C. Kimball that the Lord wants him to go on the first overseas mission of the Church. (31 years old)

1838, June 2: Son Alexander H. Smith born.

1838, November 1: Sentenced by a Missouri state militia to be shot, but the assigned executioner, Alexander W. Doniphan, refuses to carry out the murderous act.

1838, December 1: Imprisoned at Liberty Jail with several other Saints.

1839, April 16: Allowed to escape by prison guards as he and others were being transported from Liberty Jail to Columbia, Missouri.

1839, October–March 1840: Visits the president of the United States (Martin Van Buren) and members of Congress in an attempt to receive restitution for the Missouri persecutions, but is not successful.

1840-1844

1840, August 15: Publicly teaches ordinance of baptism for the dead for first time.

1841, February 4: Elected as lieutenant general of the Nauvoo Legion.

1841, November 8: Dedicates the baptismal font in the basement of the Nauvoo Temple.

1842, January 5: Opens the Red Brick Store for business in Nauvoo.

1842, February: Takes over as managing editor of the *Times and Seasons* newspaper. (36 years old)

1842, February 7: Son is stillborn.

1842, March 15: Writes a letter containing the Articles of Faith to Chicago newspaperman John Wentworth.

1842, March 17: Organizes Female Relief Society of the Church.

1842, May 4: Administers the first Nauvoo-era temple endowments on the upper floor of the Red Brick Store.

1842, May 19: Elected as mayor of the city of Nauvoo.

1843, September 28: Receives "the highest and holiest order of the priesthood" (*WJS,* 303–304). (37 years old)

1844, January 29: Announces candidacy for president of the United States of America.

1844, March: Bestows responsibility of building the Kingdom of God on the Twelve Apostles.

1844, June 18: Delivers his last public sermon. Calls out the Nauvoo Legion and declares martial law in the city for protection against mob violence.

1844, June 25: Turns himself over to Governor Thomas Ford at Carthage, Illinois, after being charged with riot and treason. The governor promises that Joseph Smith will be protected from his enemies.

1844, June 27: Murdered, along with his brother Hyrum Smith, by large, armed mob at jail in Carthage, Illinois, at approximately 5:16 P.M. (38 years old)

1844, June 29: Funeral sermon in Nauvoo, Illinois. Coffin filled with sand bags is buried in the city cemetery while the body of the Prophet is secretly buried in the basement of the Nauvoo House.

JOSEPH SMITH

The Man ❧ *The Mission* ❧ *The Message*

Other books by
MATTHEW B. BROWN

Symbols in Stone:
Symbolism on the Early Temples of the Restoration
(WITH PAUL THOMAS SMITH)

The Gate of Heaven:
Insights on the Doctrines and Symbols of the Temple

The Plan of Salvation:
Doctrinal Notes and Commentary

Plates of Gold:
The Book of Mormon Comes Forth

JOSEPH SMITH
The Man ❧ The Mission ❧ The Message

MATTHEW B. BROWN
Photography by Val W. Brinkerhoff

ACKNOWLEDGMENTS

Thanks are due to the many people and organizations that have assisted in bringing this project about. Acknowledgment is given to the Brigham Young University Museum of Art; the Harold B. Lee Library and L. Tom Perry Special Collections Library at BYU; the Daughters of the Utah Pioneers Museum in Salt Lake City; the LDS Museum of Church History and Art; the LDS Church Archives; the LDS Church Administration Building Library; the Community of Christ Archives in Independence, Missouri; the Community of Christ visitor center at the Kirtland, Ohio, Temple; the Community of Christ Nauvoo, Illinois, visitor center; the Newel K. Whitney Store historical site in Kirtland, Ohio; the artists whose works are included in this book; and the editors and graphic designers at Covenant Communications in American Fork, Utah.

Cover portrait by Danquart A. Weggeland. Photograph © Val W. Brinkerhoff. Shown courtesy of the Museum of Church History and Art, Salt Lake City, Utah. Back cover signature photograph by Val W. Brinkerhoff. Copyright © 2004 Community of Christ, used by permission.

Cover and book design copyrighted 2004 by Covenant Communications, Inc.

Published by Covenant Communications, Inc., American Fork, Utah

Printed in China
First Printing: October 2004

11 10 09 08 07 06 05   10 9 8 7 6 5 4 3 2

ISBN 1-59156-578-2

CONTENTS

FRONT AND BACK VIEWS OF A TIME-WORN
vest that once belonged to Joseph Smith Jr.
When journalist Mathew L. Davis saw
the Prophet on 5 February 1840
in Washington, D.C., he
noticed that President
Smith dressed not like a
stereotypical Old
Testament prophet (as
some imagined him), but
like an ordinary man.
Davis said, "In his garb
there are no peculiari-
ties; his dress being
that of a plain,
unpretending citi-
zen" (*WJS*, 32).

INTRODUCTION

ONE MONTH AFTER A MOB TOOK JOSEPH SMITH'S LIFE IN A JAIL IN CARTHAGE, ILLINOIS, WILLIAM W. PHELPS PUBLISHED A SONG TITLED "JOSEPH SMITH," NOW KNOWN AS "PRAISE TO THE MAN." It begins with the line "Praise to the man who communed with Jehovah" and recalls that he was "blessed to open the last dispensation" and that "he died as a martyr." The last line of Phelps's stirring composition speaks of a time when "millions shall know 'Brother Joseph' again."[1]

Some facts of Joseph Smith's life are indeed well known: he organized The Church of Jesus Christ of Latter-day Saints, he had extensive contact with heavenly beings, he received numerous revelations at their hands, and he died a martyr.

But a great many details about this man, his mission, and his message are not repeated as often or are rarely noticed. Such things include his physical appearance, his witty sense of humor, his avid love of music, his premortal identity and foreordination, his Christian discipleship, his intolerance for personal abuse, his prayers recorded in his private journal, and the last words he spoke before he died.

In the spirit of Brother Phelps's expectation that the Prophet be known again, we present text, photographs, and artwork that focus on these and other lesser-known aspects of Joseph Smith's life. Our aim is to provide the reader with a multidimensional and in-depth look at this remarkable leader revered as a prophet of God.

CHAPTER 1

Joseph Smith's EARLY YEARS

OSEPH SMITH JR. WAS BORN ON A RENTED FARM IN THE TOWN OF SHARON, VERMONT, ON 23 DECEMBER 1805.[1] At the time of his birth, his father, Joseph Smith Sr., was thirty-four years of age, and his mother, Lucy Mack Smith, was twenty-nine. Joseph Jr. entered mortality with two older brothers (Alvin and Hyrum) and one older sister (Sophronia) ahead of him; he would eventually have nine siblings in all.

Written accounts of Joseph's youth are relatively rare and their content sparse, but enough information is available to produce a sketch of what he experienced and what kind of a person he was during the early years of his life.

Joseph described his father and mother as "goodly parents,"[2] and he esteemed it "one of the greatest earthly blessings" to be raised under their benevolent care.[3] Father Smith had various occupational experiences. He was the co-owner of a mercantile store that dabbled in international trade, he labored in the cooper (or barrel-making) business, and he taught school part-time. But during young Joseph's childhood, his father found himself in "indigent circumstances" and decided to focus a great amount of his family's energy on agricultural pursuits. According to Joseph, all of the able-bodied members of his family were obliged to exert themselves during these trying times, and because of their demanding workload the children were "deprived of the benefit of an education."[4]

JOSEPH SMITH WAS BORN IN A HUMBLE LOG CABIN IN SHARON, VERMONT, IN 1805. During most of his thirty-eight and a half years, he lived in simple, rugged structures similar to this original section of his Nauvoo, Illinois, homestead (built in 1803).

Despite an initial lack of schooling, Joseph's parents believed that it was their duty to have their children properly taught. So when the Smith family moved to West Lebanon, New Hampshire, in 1812, Joseph was sent to a nearby school with one of his brothers and his sister, while his older brother Hyrum was sent off to an academy in Hanover.[5] Joseph's education was "limited to a slight acquaintance with two or three of the common branches of learning," said one of his

---

JOSEPH SMITH AND HIS SIBLINGS

ALVIN, *b. 11 February 1798*

HYRUM, *b. 9 February 1800*

SOPHRONIA, *b. 16 May 1803*

JOSEPH, *b. 23 December 1805*

SAMUEL HARRISON, *b. 14 March 1808*

EPHRAIM, *b. 13 March 1810*

WILLIAM, *b. 13 March 1811*

KATHERINE, *b. 28 July 1812*

DON CARLOS, *b. 25 March 1816*

LUCY, *b. 18 July 1821*

Joseph Fielding Smith, *Church History and Modern Revelation* (Salt Lake City: The Church of Jesus Christ of Latter-day Saints, 1946), 1:7.

---

associates. "He could read without much difficulty, and write a very imperfect hand, and had a very limited understanding of the ground rules of arithmetic."[6] It appears that Joseph Smith Jr. was an average student. A girl who attended school with him when they were children thought that he exhibited "ordinary ability" in the classroom.[7] Joseph acquired some notable public-speaking skills after he joined a debate club in Palmyra, New York,[8] but when it came to books, his mother said he was less inclined to study them than any of the other children in the family.[9] The limits of Joseph's formal education are brought to the forefront in one of his letters written in 1832. In it he excused himself for his inability to convey his ideas in writing.[10]

Joseph's mother described him as "a remarkably quiet, well-disposed child."[11] Joseph's father said that he was "an obedient son" who respected his mother's reproofs and his father's commands.[12] Joseph's brother William mentioned that he was "a truthful boy" who did not tell "crooked stories."[13] One acquaintance from outside the Smith family circle agreed with this assessment and exclaimed that "there was never a truer, purer, nobler boy than Joseph Smith."[14] This is not to say that young Joseph was perfect in every respect. Joseph himself said that between the ages of ten and twenty-one, "as is common to most or all youths, [he] fell into many vices and follies." He was quick to point out, however, that he had not been guilty of wrong-doing or injury to anybody, but "those imperfections to which [he] allude[d], and for which [he] often had occasion to lament, were a light and too often vain mind, exhibiting a foolish or trifling conversation."[15]

Growing up in an early nineteenth-century frontier environment imbued Joseph with three commendable qualities that shaped his life thereafter: a strong work ethic, patriotic fervor, and a religious nature.

STRONG WORK ETHIC

Joseph reported that during his family's stay in the Palmyra, New York, area, they engaged in "continued labor" with their hands, both at home and abroad.[16] Some of their labor at home included clearing sixty acres of heavy timber from a hundred-acre tract of land;[17] constructing split-log fences for their property; and building a one-and-a-half-story log cabin, a well, a two-story frame house, a cooper shop, a barn, and other buildings. They planted a large garden; an orchard of two hundred apple trees; and wheat, corn, flax, and beans in their fields.[18] And, of course, it was necessary to cultivate, harvest, and store all the crops that were grown.

In addition to these jobs, the Smith family also manufactured a number of goods to be sold, such as maple syrup, barrels, chairs, brooms, baskets, oilcloth covers,[19] and one thousand pounds of sugar per year.[20] They also chopped and sold cords of firewood. In all of this, said William Smith, "Joseph did his share of the work with the rest of the boys."[21]

Indeed, Joseph had earned a reputation as a dependable worker. One gentleman who lived in Palmyra often hired Joseph to work on his farm because the young man, he said,

was the best help he had ever found. He . . . always fixed the time of hoeing his large field to . . . when he could secure the services of Joseph Smith, because of the influence that boy had over the wild boys of the neighborhood, and [the man] explained that when these boys worked by themselves much time would be spent in arguing and quarreling which often ended in a ring fight. But when Joseph Smith worked with them the work went steadily forward, and he got the full worth of the wages he paid.[22]

A POCKET WATCH ONCE owned by Joseph Smith. The Prophet related in his published history that during his youth he was accustomed to rising at an early hour of the morning and attending to his chores. Some of the labors Joseph performed on his family's farm included harvesting crops, making sugar molasses, and cutting down heavy pieces of timber.

PATRIOTIC FERVOR

Both of Joseph Smith's grandfathers served in the Revolutionary War, and they passed on a strong sense of personal liberty and patriotism to their posterity. "Love of liberty was diffused into my soul by my grandfathers while they dandled me on their knees," said Joseph.[23] On one occasion the Prophet proclaimed, "It is one of the first principles of my life, and one that I have cultivated from childhood, having been

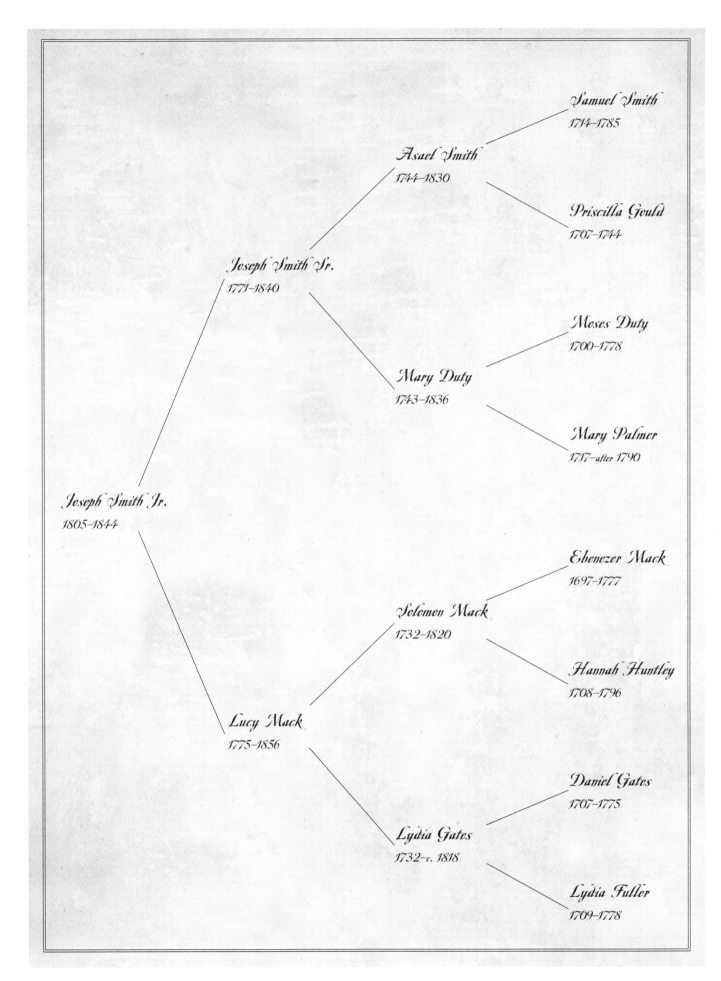

Samuel Smith
1714–1785

Asael Smith
1744–1830

Priscilla Gould
1707–1744

Joseph Smith Sr.
1771–1840

Moses Duty
1700–1778

Mary Duty
1743–1836

Mary Palmer
1717–after 1790

Joseph Smith Jr.
1805–1844

Ebenezer Mack
1697–1777

Solomon Mack
1732–1820

Hannah Huntley
1708–1796

Lucy Mack
1775–1856

Daniel Gates
1707–1775

Lydia Gates
1732–c. 1818

Lydia Fuller
1709–1778

taught it by my father, to allow everyone the liberty of conscience. I am the greatest advocate of the Constitution of the United States there is on the earth. In my feelings I am always ready to die for the protection of the weak and oppressed in their just rights."[24]

RELIGIOUS NATURE

The Prophet reported that his parents "spared no pains to instruct [him] in the Christian religion."[25] This religious training occurred at a very early age, for, as Lucy Mack Smith publicly stated, "I raised [my children] in the fear of God. When they were two or three years old I told them I wanted them to love God with all their hearts. I told them to do good."[26] This instruction took root in Joseph's heart. His mother said that as a young man Joseph "always seemed to reflect more deeply than common persons of his age upon everything of a religious nature."[27] Joseph Smith Sr. once said in blessing his son: "From thy childhood thou hast meditated much upon the great things of [the Lord's] law."[28]

The attributes ascribed to the young Joseph Smith paint a picture of a dependable boy, but they do not necessarily indicate that his childhood was anything out of the ordinary. Lucy Mack Smith stated that for the most part "nothing occurred during [Joseph's] early life, except those trivial circumstances which are common

JOSEPH SMITH'S PATERNAL LINEAGE ORIGINATED IN England, and his maternal lineage came out of Scotland. The Prophet's ancestors included a line of clergymen, a shipmaster, farmers, a schoolteacher, dissenters of organized religion, a Massachusetts state politician, a supporter of the Boston Tea Party, a highway surveyor, and participants in the Revolutionary War.

to that state of human existence."[29] However, one particular incident stands out against the background.

At the commencement of the year 1813 there was an outbreak of typhoid fever in the Connecticut River Valley. Some of the children in the Smith household came down with this illness, including seven-year-old Joseph. He eventually recovered enough so that he was able to sit up, but when he did he screamed out because of a severe pain he suddenly felt in his left shoulder.

A doctor by the name of Parker was immediately summoned to the boy's side, but the physician believed that Joseph was only suffering from a sprain. Joseph adamantly disagreed with the prognosis, as he had not previously been injured. Dr. Parker insisted that he was right and applied some bone ointment and a hot shovel, but the intense pain persisted for two more weeks.

In time the doctor discovered that a very large fever sore had formed between the left side of Joseph's chest and his left shoulder. He lanced the sore and drained about one quart of fluid. The pain disappeared from that area of the boy's body but soon relocated in the bones of his left leg and ankle. In despair Joseph cried out, "Oh father . . . the pain is so severe, how can I bear it?" His leg began to swell, and Joseph was in excruciating pain for another two weeks.

The members of Joseph's family tried all they could think of to soothe him and lessen his agony. But at the end of another week they sent for the doctor again. This time the physician thought it best to cut an eight-inch incision from Joseph's left knee to his ankle. This procedure provided Joseph with some relief, but once the wound began to heal, the pain returned. The incision was opened a second time, and again, when the wound started healing, the leg began to swell.

A council of surgeons was convened, and it was decided that the only sure remedy was the amputation of the leg. A sizable group of personnel came from Dartmouth Medical College in Hanover, New Hampshire, for the purpose of carrying out this drastic measure, but Joseph "utterly refused" to permit the operation. Mother Smith relates in her dictated history that she asked one of the surgeons, a Dr. Stone, that before they remove the entire leg they attempt to perform an experimental procedure to remove only the diseased part of the bone. She was so insistent on this point that she would not allow the doctors into her son's room until they had promised to do it. After a short consultation, the doctors agreed to carry out the experiment, and Joseph Smith reports that he gave his consent.

In preparation for this procedure, the order was given to bind Joseph to the bed with cords. But the boy was not willing to be tied down. He said decidedly, "No, doctor. I will not be bound. I can endure the procedure better unconfined."

Dr. Stone asked him, "Then will you drink some brandy?"

"No," said the young boy, "not one drop."

The doctor replied, "Will you take some wine? You must take something or you never can endure the operation to which you must be subjected."

Joseph answered,

> I will not touch one particle of liquor; neither will I be tied down. But I will tell you what I will do. I will have my father sit on the bed close by me, and then I will do anything that is necessary to be done to have the bone taken out. But mother, I want you to leave the room. I know that you cannot endure to see me suffer so. Father can bear it. . . . The Lord will help me and I shall get through with it.

Mother Smith agreed to this, and after bringing several sheets into the room for the surgeons to fold and place under Joseph's leg, she went outside and walked about one hundred yards from the house.

After exposing the diseased part of the leg bone with a blade, the surgeons bored holes directly into the bone on either side of the affected area. Then they took a pair of forceps or pincers and snapped off segments of the bad bone. The resulting pain was excruciating. Joseph screamed loudly as sweat rolled off his face, and his features contorted in expressions of indescribable agony. Mother Smith heard his cries and rushed to the side of her son twice during his ordeal. The first time she entered the room, Joseph told her to go back outside and he would tough it out. The second time she entered, Joseph's leg and the bed were covered in blood, and the doctors had to forcibly remove her from the room and have her detained.

Fortunately, the operation was successful, and Joseph's leg did not have to be removed. As the leg healed, Joseph lost a substantial amount of weight, and over time fourteen bone splinters eventually worked their way out of his wound. He was sent to live with his uncle Jesse Smith in Salem, Massachusetts, in the hope that the ocean breezes would benefit him, and there he recovered his health and strength. He did, however, have to use crutches until the year 1817.[30]

In this experience Joseph demonstrated incredible fortitude and maturity for one so young. He showed compassion for his mother and unusual trust in his father and in the Lord. The resolve and conviction with which he met this early trial give a glimpse of the man he would become.

JOSEPH SMITH WAS raised in a religious home, where he was taught the truths of the Bible. The Prophet purchased this pulpit-style copy of the King James Version (which includes the Apocrypha) for $3.75 at E. B. Grandin's Palmyra, New York, bookstore in October 1829. He subsequently utilized this volume of scripture (between 1830 and 1833) as he produced an inspired translation of the Old and New Testaments.

AFTER THREE SUCCESSIVE CROP FAILURES IN NORWICH, VERMONT, JOSEPH SMITH'S FATHER TRAVELED ALONE to western New York in the hope of finding better land and climatic conditions. He decided that the village of Palmyra (which was adjacent to the Erie Canal) presented the best prospects and sent for his family. Mother Smith and her children made the journey to New York in 1816 and had a joyful reunion with Father Smith, as depicted in this painting by Paul Mann.

CHAPTER 2

APPEARANCE
& Personality

NO GENUINE PHOTOGRAPHIC IMAGE OF THE PROPHET JOSEPH SMITH IS KNOWN TO EXIST, AND BECAUSE HE LIVED IN THE FIRST HALF OF THE NINETEENTH CENTURY, NO RECORDING OF HIS VOICE WAS EVER MADE. Yet even without these types of primary resources, it is possible to piece together a sharp and revealing picture of how the Prophet looked and acted. The historical sources brought together here reveal the portrait of a man with an impressive appearance as well as a keen mind and agreeable personality.

APPEARANCE

A surprising number of people who became acquainted with the Prophet Joseph Smith left behind written descriptions of his physical appearance. No less surprising is the amount of detail that can be found in these accounts.

In 1844 a reporter from St. Louis met with the Prophet for the specific purpose of producing a verbal sketch of his person. The reporter listed interesting details about the appearance of the Prophet's head. "The shape of his head is a very oblong oval—the coronal region high . . . and the frontal retreating. . . . His forehead is . . . without a furrow, and . . . somewhat symmetrical. His . . . cheeks [are] full."[1] James Palmer, who was well acquainted with the Prophet during the Nauvoo era of Church history, recollected that from a side view his chin was "a little tipped," or sloping.[2]

THIS OIL PORTRAIT, DONE FROM LIFE IN SEPTEMBER 1842, IS ACCREDITED TO David W. Rogers of New York. It is one of the few images that compares closely with a cast made of the Prophet's face in 1844 and is thus considered to be an accurate reflection of his likeness.

Descriptions of President Smith's skin are nearly unanimous in stating that he had a fair or light complexion.[3] Bathsheba W. Smith described the texture and tone of his skin as being "very nice."[4] One source says that his skin was "white,"[5] while another relates that "his face seemed almost colorless."[6]

"His hair is quite light and fine," said a newspaper report in 1844.[7] One woman referred to its hue as "golden brown."[8] Stephen Harding noted that Joseph's hair color had changed over the course of time. It had "turned from tow-colored" (or light blond) in his youth to "light auburn" in his more mature years.[9] He had "the longest, thickest, light [eye]lashes you ever saw," said one observer, and his "[eye]brows [were] also light and thick—indeed, precisely of that description called beetle-brow."[10] Parley P. Pratt stated that the

Stephen S. Harding recalled that sometime before the fall of 1827 he had seen Joseph Smith fishing in the pond at Durfee's gristmill in Palmyra, New York. He described Joseph as a boy three years his senior who had tow-colored hair and long legs.

See Thomas Gregg, *The Prophet of Palmyra* (New York: John B. Alden, 1890), 36.

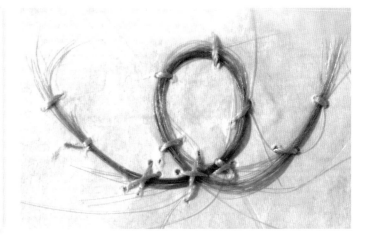

Prophet had "very little beard,"[11] and so he was normally clean-shaven, or, as James Palmer phrased it, "he wore no whiskers."[12]

Josiah Quincy reported after meeting with Joseph Smith that he had "blue eyes standing prominently out upon his light complexion."[13] The ball of each eye was "full and round," according to Zina Young.[14] Charlotte Haven recalled that his eyes were "set far back in the head."[15] Some people noticed that Joseph's eyes had a sharp or bright quality to them and could thus be compared to those of an eagle,[16] while others saw intelligence beaming out from behind them.[17] Parley P. Pratt remembered that the Prophet had a serene, steady, yet penetrating glance.[18]

Nobody could help but notice Joseph Smith's nose, because, as one observer matter-of-factly declared, it was "prominent."[19] It is described by others as being "long and straight,"[20] somewhat heavy in appearance,[21] and similar to those seen in the culture of the ancient Romans.[22]

His mouth was "massive," according to one observer,[23] and even though his upper lip was evidently "full and rather protruding,"[24] he had relatively thin lips.[25] One person mentioned in print that Joseph had a frequent and agreeable smile and that in normal conversation his voice was "low and soft."[26] But when it came time to speak outdoors to large crowds, says another source, he was able to project his voice to the point where it sounded "like the roaring of many waters."[27] Benjamin F. Johnson reported that there was a slight whistling sound to the Prophet's speech because a mob had broken off a piece of one of his front teeth during an attack in 1832.[28]

In his recollection of the upper part of the Prophet's body, James Palmer said that he had "a large, full chest."[29] Other people thought that his shoulders were broad[30] and very rounded[31]—though not so much as Brigham Young's[32]—and his shoulders were also a little bit stooped.[33]

Joseph Smith was "a very strongly built man," according to Homer Duncan;[34] and the governor of Illinois, Thomas Ford, reported that the Prophet was "uncommonly well muscled."[35] Joseph's prominent musculature was undoubtedly built during many years of chopping and hauling wood, quarrying and moving stone, planting and harvesting crops, and constructing buildings on the American frontier. It is interesting to

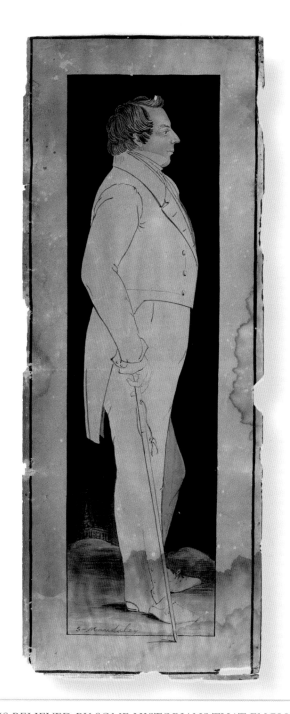

IT IS BELIEVED BY SOME HISTORIANS THAT ENGLISH portraitist Sutcliffe Maudsley rendered this ink drawing of Joseph Smith sometime between 1842 and 1844. It hung in the Mansion House in Nauvoo, Illinois, for a number of years. A small representation of the Nauvoo Temple can be seen to the left of the Prophet's legs.

(OPPOSITE) THIS LOCK OF JOSEPH SMITH'S LIGHT brown hair was cut in the kitchen of his home and given to Henrietta K. Whitney, one of his neighbors, as a memento.

(OPPOSITE) THIS ETCHED SILVER SPECTACLE CASE has been identified as belonging to Joseph Smith. The Prophet did in fact own a pair of spectacles, but they were not for practical use. The lenses were made of ordinary glass (see *Ensign*, January 1984, 36).

JOSEPH SMITH'S STOVEPIPE HAT. IT IS REPORTED BY one observer that President Smith, while traveling on horseback, stored papers in the hollow of his "tall black hat" (*Juvenile Instructor*, vol. 27, no. 6, 15 March 1892, 174).

ONE OF JOSEPH'S WOODEN WALKING CANES. JOSEPH walked with a limp during his adult years as the result of a childhood leg operation, but it is nowhere stated that he needed the assistance of a cane. This walking stick is, therefore, probably more fashionable than practical.

note that the Prophet's hands were apparently "quite small for his proportions."[36] Yet several individuals mentioned that when Joseph took them by the hand, the clasp was a cordial one.[37]

Stephen Harding wrote that the Prophet was "what might be termed long legged, and [he had] big feet."[38] In fact, his feet are described by one observer as being "massive . . . and extensive."[39] After undergoing the agonizing operation on his leg, as noted, he got around on crutches for about four years. The Prophet recounted that when he was twelve years of age it was excruciatingly painful for him to walk for long distances, and such efforts made him very weary.[40]

Joseph Smith is characterized as having a tall, well-built form[41] and presenting "a very formidable appearance."[42] One of Joseph Smith's uncles stated that he "stood [an] even six feet high in his stocking feet."[43] Another source indicates that by 1842 he weighed "two hundred and twelve pounds."[44] It was the opinion of several people that the Prophet tended somewhat to corpulency.[45]

Several sources mention that Joseph Smith was considered to be handsome[46] and also state that he was "a young looking man of his age."[47]

Some who knew the Prophet commented on his countenance. Emmeline B. Wells remarked that "his expression was mild and almost childlike in repose."[48] And, indeed, Parley P. Pratt concurred, saying that "his countenance was ever mild," but he added that it was also "affable, beaming with intelligence and benevolence; mingled with a look of interest and an unconscious smile, or cheerfulness; and entirely free from all restraint or affectation of gravity."[49] Others saw something of an otherworldly nature when they looked at their Church leader's face. From the perspective of John Hess, "there was something heavenly and angelic in his looks that [he] never witnessed in the countenance of any other person."[50] Such descriptions of Joseph's countenance accord well with contemporary assessments of his personality.

PERSONALITY

Joseph Smith's nature is revealed in his own statements about himself and also in the statements of friends and acquaintances who speak of his general disposition, mental faculties, and manner of speech.

GENERAL DISPOSITION

Joseph publicly declared that he was a "playful and cheerful" kind of a person.[51] This self-assessment is confirmed by Elias Cox, who said that the Prophet "had a very pleasant disposition and always seemed to be happy."[52] Thomas Ford, the governor of Illinois, wrote that Joseph Smith was "full of levity, even to boyish romping."[53]

Historical records indicate that the Prophet "often indulged in harmless jokes" with his "most familiar friends."[54] Benjamin F. Johnson—a friend of Joseph's since boyhood—was once holding nine silver dollars. Joseph playfully hit the bottom of his hand and scattered the money all over the floor. Benjamin responded by engaging him in a wrestling bout.[55]

Joseph Smith could also "crack a joke," said Jacob Jones.[56] The *History of the Church* preserves an amusing recital of one of these jokes, told in May 1843. When the Prophet was standing before the Nauvoo Legion militia, he called out for a glass of water. He then said to the assembled soldiers,

> I will drink you a toast, to the overthrow of the mobocrats. . . . Here's wishing they were in the middle of the sea in a stone canoe, with iron paddles, and a shark swallow the canoe and the devil swallow the shark and him locked up in the northwest corner of hell, the key lost and a blind man looking for it.[57]

On other occasions the Prophet exhibited a more subtle sense of humor. Once two boys were fighting in the streets of Nauvoo, and Joseph ran outside to put a stop to it. He grabbed the young combatants by their shirt collars and informed them that it was illegal for anybody in the city to fight except for him—the mayor. He then told them that the next time they felt inclined to engage in a brawl they would have to go down to his house and ask him for one. The lecture effectively

Peter Burnett, a non-Mormon who became the first governor of California, said of Joseph,

He possessed the most indomitable perseverance, and was a good judge of men, and deemed himself born to command, and he did command. His views were so strange and striking, and his manner was so earnest, and apparently so candid, that you could not but be interested. There was a kind, familiar look about him, that pleased you. He was very courteous in discussion, readily admitting what he did not intend to controvert, and would not oppose you abruptly, but had due deference to your feelings.

Peter H. Burnett, *An Old California Pioneer* (Oakland, CA.: Biobooks, 1946), 40.

curbed the boy's enthusiasm for fighting.[58] In another incident, President Smith said that he was going to "study in some law books and become a great lawyer." He then proceeded to "put his head down on [a] law book and fall asleep." He then "went to snoring."[59]

This is not to say that Joseph Smith never experienced anxiety, sorrow, or concern. Emily Partridge Young reported: "I have known him to come in with his head bowed. He would walk the floor back and forth, with his hands clasped behind him (a way he had of placing his hands when his mind was deeply troubled), his countenance showing that he was weighed down with some terrible burden."[60] Daniel Tyler saw tears running down the Prophet's face after his brother William Smith had publicly denounced him.[61] And Joseph wrote of the "great anxiety" he felt while he was away from his wife and children.[62]

On the whole, however, Joseph seems to have kept a light heart, even with the trials that came with his calling. Indeed, Joseph's merry manner was quite at odds with the behavior of most religious leaders during the early nineteenth century. The Prophet rejected the notion that a person was not truly pious who did not display a "super-abundant stock of sanctimoniousness"—

complete with long-faced expression and drawn-out, donkeylike tone of voice.[63] He explained his noncompliance with this particular standard of piety by saying that he did not wish to be considered "a great deal better than anybody else."[64]

The Saints in the early days of the Church often referred to the Prophet as "Brother Joseph," and this was partly because he had such an open and friendly disposition. William Appleby made note of this in 1841 when he wrote, "You may ask him any question you please, in a becoming manner, concerning his private history, his revelations, the dealings of the Lord towards him, his politics, faith, hope, or whatever else that is consistent or reasonable to propose, and he will answer you as becomes a gentleman, even a Saint!"[65]

MENTAL FACULTIES

Joseph's associates reveal that he had not only a pleasant personality but also impressive mental depth. Peter Burnett, for instance, recalled that "he had the capacity for discussing a subject in many different aspects, and for proposing many original views, even of ordinary matters."[66] William Clayton wrote to an acquaintance in England, "We have had the privilege of conversing with Joseph Smith Jr. and . . . he is *not* an idiot [as evil reports about him claim], but a man of sound judgment, and possessed of abundance of intelligence, and whilst you listen to his conversation you receive intelligence which expands your mind and causes your heart to rejoice."[67] One of the Prophet's clerks reported an incident when someone attempted to determine just how much depth the latter-day seer's mind had. He stated, "Among other great men who called to see him was Cyrus Walker—a lawyer of much note; he tried to sound the Prophet, and see how deep he was. Well, it was with Walker as it had been with all the others; he soon got enough, found Joseph too deep for his lead and line, and gave up the enterprise."[68]

Some people recognized that Joseph Smith was "possessed of a mind of contemplative and reflective character."[69] His own mother reported that even as a young man he was given to "deep study" and thought.[70] And he

used his mind for analytical purposes as well. He was "a comparative man," said Brigham Young, "regarding everything according to the circumstances of the case, and every person according to their intrinsic worth."[71]

The type of thoughts that Joseph Smith fostered in his mind are enumerated in the observations of several individuals. "He loved innocence and purity," said Louisa Littlefield.[72] Edwin Rushton saw that when a

A RICHLY COLORED PATCHWORK QUILT DISPLAYED in the master bedroom of the Prophet's Nauvoo Mansion House. This unique artifact was reportedly made by Emma Smith from the clothing of the Church's President (Joseph) and Patriarch (Hyrum) after they had been martyred at Carthage Jail in June 1844.

person was "in conversation with him there was nothing frivolous, light-minded, or debasing."[73] Samuel Miles likewise related that the Prophet had "a firm dislike of that which was degrading."[74] One incident, in particular, illustrates the disdain that he felt for persons of questionable character. After the Mansion House in Nauvoo opened its hotel wing in the fall of 1843, a man who had registered there insulted one of the hired girls. After the man retired for the evening, Joseph was informed about what had taken place, and the next morning he met the man as he came down the stairs. Joseph said to him,

"Sir: I understand that you insulted one of the employees of this house last evening." [The man] began to make all kinds of apologies, but

nothing of this kind would answer the purpose. [Joseph] told the stranger to get his baggage and to get away from there as soon as possible, in such unmistakable language, and in a tone of voice that almost made [the man's] hair stand straight on his head. The man offered to pay his bill [but the Prophet replied,] "I want you to get [out]. I want none of your money, or any other man's of your stamp." Upon this the stranger cut a lively exit.[75]

MANNER OF SPEECH

Another way in which the Prophet's personality was manifested was through his distinctive manner of speech. Both Lorenzo Snow and Jared Carter acknowledged that Joseph Smith was not a naturally gifted speaker.[76] One of Joseph's acquaintances described his style of delivery as "awkward,"[77] and, indeed, Joseph described himself as "a stuttering sort of a boy,"[78] probably meaning that he sometimes stammered or hesitated when he spoke. Nevertheless, people like Enoch Dodge, who heard Joseph preach many times, thought that "he was truly a great speaker."[79]

It is known that Joseph Smith occasionally practiced his public-speaking skills with a small group of trusted friends,[80] and he had some definite views on how a person should act while in front of an audience. He told his brother Don Carlos Smith that a "speaker should always speak in his natural tone of voice, and not . . . keep in one loud strain, but . . . act without affectation" or showiness.[81] He also believed that simplicity in discourse was a virtue. He told one of the crowds that sat before him, "I do not calculate or intend to please your ears with superfluity of words or oratory, or with much learning; but I calculate to edify you with the simple truths from heaven."[82] The Prophet had an appreciable talent for doing this, for, as George W. Taggart wrote, "The information which comes out of his mouth . . . is not in big words . . . but that which anyone can understand."[83] Brigham Young observed that President Smith "took heaven, figuratively speaking, and brought it down to earth; and he took the earth, brought it up, and opened up, in plainness and simplicity, the things of God."[84]

How did the Prophet sound when he was speaking? Mathew Davis, who heard him talk in Washington, D.C., reported, "Everything he says, is said in a manner

Lorenzo Snow first met the Prophet in 1832. They met again in June 1836 when Lorenzo was invited to dinner at Joseph's home in Kirtland. Of the second meeting Lorenzo said,

He seemed to have changed considerably in his appearance since I first saw him at Hiram, four and a half years before. He was very ready in conversation, and had apparently lost that reserve and diffident feeling that he seemed to have before. He was free and easy in his conversation with me, making me feel perfectly at home in his presence. In fact, I felt as free with him as if we had been special friends for years. He was very familiar.

Improvement Era, vol. 40, no. 2, February 1937, 83.

to leave an impression that he is sincere."[85] At another gathering George A. Smith heard him speak "very freely [for] about one hour . . . ; his manner and style were very unassuming and affable."[86] And in Christopher Crary's judgment, "his language . . . was correct, forcible, . . . right to the point and convincing."[87] Parley P. Pratt provided a detailed and insightful assessment of the Prophet's speaking skills, which bears repeating here.

His language [was] abounding in original eloquence peculiar to himself—not polished—not studied—not smooth and softened by education and refined by art; but flowing forth in its own native simplicity, and profusely abounding in variety of subject and manner. He interested and edified while, at the same time, he amused and entertained his audience; and none listened to him that were ever weary with his discourse. I have known him to retain a congregation of willing and anxious listeners for many hours together, in the midst of cold or sunshine, rain or wind, while they were laughing at one moment and weeping the next. Even his most bitter enemies were generally overcome, if he could once get their ears.[88]

There were times when Joseph Smith's speaking abilities went noticeably beyond their natural limitations. "At times he was filled with the Holy Ghost," said Lorenzo Snow, "speaking as with the voice of an archangel and filled with the power of God." On such occasions "his whole person shone and his face was lightened until it appeared as the whiteness of the driven snow."[89] The presence of this spiritual power added potency to Joseph's utterances, as when Mary Ann Winters "stood close by the Prophet while he was preaching . . . in the grove by the temple. The Holy Spirit lighted up his countenance till it glowed like a halo around him, and his words penetrated the hearts of all who heard him."[90] Such portrayals of the Prophet do much to explain the intense love and loyalty he inspired in the Saints and others who knew him.

HEBREW GRAMMAR book used in the School of the Prophets. Joseph Smith had little formal education during his younger years and was consequently looked upon by some people as being illiterate. But as Joseph grew older, he sought after educational opportunities and studied subjects such as grammar, philosophy, literature, and politics. The Prophet's mother told one man, "You don't know what a brain my boy has under that old hat" (*St. Louis Globe-Democrat,* 21 February 1897, 34).

IN THIS PAINTING BY WILLIAM MAJOR, JOSEPH SMITH is shown in council with other Church leaders (left to right: Hyrum Smith, Willard Richards, Joseph Smith, Orson Pratt, Parley P. Pratt, Orson Hyde, Heber C. Kimball, and Brigham Young). It was one of the Prophet's duties to teach doctrine to the elders, and they in turn were to teach doctrine to the Latter-day Saints (see *HC*, 6:319).

CHAPTER 3

The PROPHET'S CHARACTER

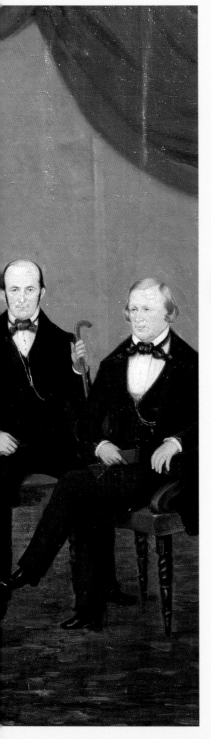

THE CHARACTER OF JOSEPH SMITH IS A SUBJECT OF GREAT INTEREST AMONG ADHERENTS OF THE RELIGION HE HELPED TO RESTORE AND A MATTER OF INTENSE DEBATE AMONG HIS DETRACTORS. Fortunately, written descriptions of the Prophet's character traits have been preserved. His own words and the words of individuals who had more than just a passing acquaintance indicate he was an admirable man who was nevertheless thoroughly human.

IMPERFECT

Perhaps one of the most revealing, and commendable, things about Joseph Smith's character was that he was willing to acknowledge his imperfections. He told the Latter-day Saints in October 1842 that he was only a man who had "infirmities" and that they should not expect him to be perfect.[1] He once published a notice in the Church's official periodical declaring, "I do not, nor never have, pretended to be any other than a man 'subject to passion,' and liable, without the assisting grace of the Savior, to deviate from that perfect path in which all men are commanded to walk!"[2] And on another occasion he compared himself to ancient men of God, saying, "Although I was called of my Heavenly Father to lay the foundation of this great work and kingdom in this dispensation, and testify of His revealed will to scattered Israel, I am subject to like passions as other men, like the prophets of olden times."[3] Yet even with these acknowledgments, he made it clear that he was willing at all times to give up any fault so that the Saints would have a virtuous leader.[4]

ORDERLY

Imperfect as he may have been, Joseph Smith could not be faulted for being untidy. Jesse W. Crosby made note of the fact that Joseph Smith was not a jumbled or cluttered kind of a person; rather, he was orderly in his habits.

> [H]e always left his fence clear of everything that might gather fire, such as underbrush, loose limbs, and tall strong weeds. He was orderly. His wood yard was an example of order. Logs were neatly piled and all trash cleared away. If he did not finish the log on which he was chopping, the remnant was laid back on the pile and not left on the ground for a stumbling block. The chips he made he picked up himself into a basket and put them in a wood box which stood in the wood yard.[5]

HARDWORKING

Joseph's enemies tried to convince the general public through the press and the rumor mill that he was a lazy man who sponged off others for a living.

But this could hardly be more untrue. "He was a laboring man," remembered Wilford Woodruff, "and gained his bread by the sweat of his brow."[6] Indeed, there are numerous accounts of Joseph engaging in hard physical labor (like hoeing corn and potatoes or harvesting wheat) in order to sustain his immediate and extended families. And it wasn't just sporadic, short-term labor, either. William H. Walker reported

that he "went into the hayfield with him, and he assisted in mowing grass, with a scythe, many a day, putting in ten hours good hard work. Very few if any, were his superior in that kind of work."[7] He was so strong and active, according to another person, that he could build more rods of good fence in one day than most men could in two.[8]

THE STANNARD STONE QUARRY, FROM WHICH ROCKS were hewn to build the House of the Lord in Kirtland, Ohio, was located about two miles south of the temple building site. It was not uncommon to see the Prophet Joseph Smith laboring along-side the Saints in this quarry. Notice the channels in the rock where sections of stone have been chiseled away.

THIS PITCHER AND BASIN BELONGED TO JOSEPH AND EMMA SMITH AND IS SEEN HERE INSIDE THEIR Nauvoo homestead. Joseph assisted in the care of his children, and it is not hard to imagine him washing them off after they had spent the day playing along the banks of the Mississippi River.

HELPFUL

Joseph's commendable work ethic extended beyond his immediate circle, for he was inclined to help others. He could be seen cutting timber and quarrying stone to build the temples of God[9] or caring for widowed Saints by personally helping to build houses for them to live in.[10] There is ample evidence that despite his divine calling and heavy responsibilities, he did not consider himself to be above doing everyday household chores. Jesse W. Crosby, for instance, observed the Prophet "building kitchen fires, carrying out ashes, carrying in wood and water, [and] assisting in the care of the children."[11]

When the members of Zion's Camp were headed toward Independence, Missouri, in an attempt to redeem property stolen from the Saints by barbaric mobs, there were times when their wagons got bogged down in swampy terrain. Invariably, Joseph was the first man hauling on the ropes to pull the wagons out. Significantly, John Chidester recalled that "this was characteristic of him in all times of difficulty."[12]

Joseph also assisted others in understanding the doctrines of the kingdom. Wandle Mace related that sometimes the Prophet would attend a Nauvoo lyceum, or lecturing school, that convened during the wintertime. Eighteen attendees were given a turn at discussing different gospel subjects, and even though each of the participants had his own way of handling the subject, there was no discord, jarring, or contention. In fact, Wandle said that these gatherings were instructive, entertaining, and edifying for those who were involved. Joseph attended these meetings whenever practicable, and in addition to giving his encouragement he offered instruction and assistance. Said he, "Get into your lyceums, and investigate doctrine, and if you run against a snag, I am here, I will help you off."[13]

INTOLERANT OF ABUSE

Though helpful and kind, the Prophet was not one to sit quietly by while individuals took advantage of him or even heaped abuse upon his head. He once published a notice in the Church's newspaper to politely "inform" his friends and anybody else that wanted to write to him that they would have to pay for their own postage! He was evidently having an ongoing problem with collect-on-delivery charges.[14]

The Prophet's name was continually being vilified in the public press, but one editor in particular, Thomas Sharp of Warsaw, Illinois, was especially foul in the accusations he made. When Joseph couldn't tolerate the harsh content of Sharp's paper any longer, he canceled his subscription and attached a note that read: "Discontinue my paper—its contents are calculated to pollute me—to patronize the filthy sheet—that tissue of lies—that sink in iniquity—is disgraceful to any moral man."[15]

After a personal meeting with Joseph,
a non-Mormon newspaper reporter wrote,

*We had supposed from the stories
and statements we had read of "Jo Smith"
(as he is termed in the papers) to find him
a very illiterate, uncouth sort of a man;
but from a long conversation,
we acknowledge an agreeable disappointment.
In conversation, he appears intelligent and
candid, and divested of all malicious thought
and feeling towards his relentless persecutors.*

Quincy Whig, vol. 1, no. 52, 27 April 1839.

Joseph F. Smith, the Prophet's nephew, told of an incident that bears full recital because it shows that even though Joseph Smith was called a kind man by those who knew him well, he had his limitations when it came to people who showed him contemptuous disrespect.

I will tell you a little circumstance that I saw myself. . . . I was one day playing marbles in front of the Mansion [House in Nauvoo, Illinois,] with my cousin Alexander Smith. We were amusing ourselves on the sidewalk. The fence ran along within six or eight feet of the door of the Mansion, and we were playing at the gate just outside the stone steps, when all of a sudden the door flew open and I looked, and there came a great, big man [named Josiah Butterfield] right off the end of Joseph Smith's foot, and he lit on the sidewalk just by the gate.

I saw that myself. Well, I wondered what in the world was the matter. Since I grew to be a man, I learned that this man was there insulting the Prophet, and abusing him in his own house, until the Prophet thought he had stood enough abuse from him, so he opened his door and invited him out; that he did not go as quickly as the Prophet wanted him to go, and he gave him the assistance of his boot, and helped him out.[16]

HONORABLE

In the estimation of Lorenzo Snow and Parley P. Pratt, "there never was a man who possessed a higher degree of integrity" than Joseph Smith.[17] There are several examples that bear this assessment out. Jesse W. Crosby, for instance, remarked that Joseph had an

AFTER RUTHLESS MOBS DROVE THE LATTER-DAY Saints from Missouri, some of them kidnapped Joseph Smith's friend Orrin Porter Rockwell. The Prophet borrowed money in the hope of setting him free and went to great lengths to pay the lender back at the appointed time.

"unfailing habit" of always sharpening an ax before returning it to the person he had borrowed it from, and if he borrowed a sack of flour from somebody he always repaid the debt with more flour than he had first received. His philosophy was that "anything borrowed should be returned always with interest to the lender."[18]

A story told by Sarah Pomeroy illustrates the lengths to which Joseph would go to keep his good name and reputation intact.

The Prophet had been falsely accused of an attempt to murder Governor Boggs of Missouri. The mobbers had tried every means to take him, and had made their boast that if they got him, he never should return alive. Porter Rockwell, a firm friend of Joseph's, had been kidnapped and taken to Missouri as an accomplice, and was about to have his trial, but money was scarce wherewith to pay the lawyers' fees. Joseph requested my father to lend him $100.00 to pay the lawyer who defended Porter Rockwell. He explained the

situation, and father freely counted out the money. "This shall be returned within three days, if I am alive," said the Prophet, and departed.

My aunt, father's sister, who was camped with us, was quite wrathy, and called my father very foolish and unwise.

"Don't you know, Thomas," said she, "you will never see a cent of that money again. Here are your family without a home, and you throw your money away."

"Don't worry, Katie," father replied, "if he cannot pay it, he is welcome to it."

This conversation was held before us children, and I thought seriously about it. Would he pay it, or would he not? But I had strong faith that he would.

The day came when it was to be paid. A cold, wet, rainy day. The day passed. Night came; 9 o'clock, 10 o'clock, and we all retired for the night. Shortly after there was a knock at the door. Father arose and went to it, and there in the driving rain stood the Prophet Joseph.

"Here, Brother Thomas, is the money." A light was struck, and seated at the table, he counted out the $100.00 in gold.

He said, "Brother Thomas, I have been trying all day to raise this sum, for my honor was at stake."[19]

HUMBLE

Joseph Smith taught the Latter-day Saints that it was necessary to show humility and meekness before the Lord,[20] and he was a practitioner of the doctrine that he preached. "He was a very humble and meek man," said David Whitmer,[21] and it was the opinion of Eliza R. Snow that "he was humble as a little child."[22] Jane Snyder remembered that as a "seer and revelator he was fearless and outspoken, yet humble, never considering that he was more than the mouthpiece through whom God spoke."[23] And in a letter to a friend, Mary Fielding wrote, "He feels himself to be but a poor creature and can do nothing but what God enables him to do."[24] It was not uncommon for the Prophet to characterize himself in private correspondences, public communications, and Church-related documents as "Your humble servant."

RELIGIOUSLY DEVOTED

One would expect that the leader of the restored church would be a religiously devoted person. But as some of Joseph Smith's more caustic critics deny him such a distinction, it is important to establish the fact. One way to go about doing this is to examine his activities when he was out of public view and thus unlikely to be putting on a show for the benefit of his reputation.

We first turn to Martin Harris, who often employed Joseph on his farm in Palmyra, New York. He stated that during the time they spent together "the Prophet was devoted and attentive to his prayers."[25] Eliza R. Snow also reported that "three times a day he had family worship" in his Nauvoo, Illinois, home.[26]

William Walker was a witness to the Church president's private devotions when he was sent to Nauvoo to conduct some business in the spring of 1840. As he approached Joseph's homestead at nine in the evening, he heard the family singing. "I thought I had never heard such sweet, heavenly music before," said William. And he was "equally interested in the prayer offered by the Prophet."[27] Orson Pratt was another individual who personally observed these religious activities. He boarded at the Prophet's home over an extended period of time and "knew him . . . as a private citizen." His morning and evening devotions, recalled Orson, were both "earnest and humble."[28]

Once when Joseph Smith was away from his home on Church business, he wrote a letter to his wife, Emma, and informed her that in his spare time he visited a grove of trees in back of the town where he was staying. There, in seclusion, he would "give vent to all the feelings of [his] heart in meditation and prayer."[29] The kind of prayers that could be found in the Prophet's heart were such as these:

"I ask God, in the name of Jesus Christ, to . . . bless me with much wisdom and understanding, and dispose of me to the best advantage for my brethren, and the advancement of Thy cause and kingdom."

"O may God . . . end[ow] me with qualifications to magnify His name while I live."

"O Lord glorify Thyself. Thy will be done and not mine."

"O Lord, may Thy Holy Spirit be with Thy servants forever. Amen."[30]

CHAPTER 4

Enjoyments & TRIALS

ASIDE FROM HIS CALLING AS THE FIRST PROPHET OF THE FINAL GOSPEL DISPENSATION, JOSEPH SMITH WAS IN MANY WAYS JUST LIKE OTHER MEN. During his time on the earth he experienced both the good and the bad that mortality brings. Most of the joys and trials he met in life were not unlike those of other individuals, while some of the experiences he went through were far from ordinary.

ENJOYMENTS

FAMILY

One of Joseph Smith's chiefest joys in life was the love that he shared with his family. The Smith household was a rather large one. Emma bore Joseph eight sons and one daughter in all (some of whom died young), and they adopted a pair of twins (a boy and a girl) after the infants' mother passed away in 1831.

The Prophet noted in his published history that being at home with his family brought him "great joy."[1] The close bond he felt with them is illustrated in a letter, written in January 1840, wherein he said his heart was "entwined around" his wife and his children. He wanted them to remember his love for each of them and to know that he did not enjoy being deprived of their society.[2] On occasions when the

---

JOSEPH SMITH ENJOYED PLAYING A WIDE VARIETY OF NINETEENTH-CENTURY sports and games, including wrestling, baseball, and checkers.

Prophet was away from home on Church business, he specifically petitioned the Lord to let His blessings rest upon the Smith family[3] and even grant them health and long life so they could do good in their generation for Christ's sake.[4]

Joseph engaged in many activities that strengthened the bonds of his family. He noted that one day he enjoyed just sitting around the fireside and socializing with his wife and children.[5] On another occasion he took his family on a ride down the Mississippi River on a steamboat, and they were entertained on their journey by a fine band of musicians.[6] Sometimes the Prophet could be seen playing with his children;[7] at

JOSEPH SMITH HAD A heartfelt relationship with each member of his immediate family. This was especially the case with his wife Emma (pictured above). The letter pictured here, written in 1832 while the Prophet was away on Church business, ends with the words, "You must comfort yourself knowing that God is your friend in heaven and that you have one true and living friend on earth— your husband, Joseph Smith, Jr."

other times he would read to them, take them on pleasure rides in his carriage, accompany them to the circus, or go sliding on the frozen river or duck hunting one-on-one with a son.[8]

John Bernhisel, who stayed for a time as a boarder at the Nauvoo Mansion House, observed that the Prophet was both a "tender and affectionate husband and parent."[9] And Benjamin F. Johnson was so impressed by the love that the Prophet exhibited toward members of his family that, in his opinion, Joseph's devotion as a husband and father "stopped only at idolatry."[10]

ATHLETICS

Joseph Smith was a very athletic man, and he enjoyed activities of a competitive nature. According to John Murdock, the Prophet "scarcely ever met his equal as an athlete."[11] There are records of him running footraces, jumping for distance with his feet placed at a mark, and high-jumping over corral fences.[12] He also enjoyed a game called pulling sticks, which he played in his office at the Mansion House. In this sport, two people sit on the ground, each with his feet pressed against the feet of the other, and they grasp a stick situated between them. The object is to exert enough force to pull the other person up to a standing position. Joseph Smith was so strong that he could pull some people up with just one hand.[13]

Joseph also liked to play a nineteenth-century form of baseball. "Joseph would always conform to the rules," said Aroet Hale. "He would catch till it came his turn to take the club. Then, being a very stout man he would knock the ball so far that we used to holl[er] to the boy that was going for the ball to take his dinner. This used to make the Prophet laugh."[14]

Perhaps the Prophet's favorite sport was wrestling. His father, Joseph Smith Sr., was a famed wrestler when he was a young man, and this is likely the reason the younger Joseph had such a love for the sport.[15] It is said that President Smith "would leave a meal at any time to wrestle with anyone"[16] and was above average in his skill.[17] Apparently, he also had considerable stamina. A story handed down by one Nauvoo family reports that he would occasionally wrestle for an hour at a time.[18]

One of the Church's official clerks, Howard Coray, recalled a wrestling incident with Joseph that got a little out of hand. He wrote,

The Prophet and [I], after looking at his horses, and admiring them, . . . were just across the road from his house [and] we started thither, the Prophet at this same time put[ting] his arm over my shoulder. When we had reached about the middle of the road, he stopped and remarked, "Brother Coray, I wish you were a little larger, I would like to have some fun with you." I replied, "Perhaps you can as it is," not realizing what I was saying. Joseph, a man of over 200 pounds weight, while I scarcely 130 pounds, made it not a little ridiculous for me to think of engaging with him in anything like a scuffle. However, as soon as I made this reply he began to trip me; he took some kind of a lock on my right leg, from which I was unable to extricate it, and throwing me around, broke it some three inches above the ankle joint. He immediately carried me into the house, pulled off my boot, and found at once that my leg was decidedly broken; then he got some splinters and bandaged it. A number of times that day did he come in to see me, endeavoring to console me as much as possible.[19]

On 18 February 1843 the Quorum of the Twelve Apostles sent a letter out to some of the Saints, reminding them that the Prophet's persecutors had recently "relieved him of his property" and he was therefore forced to set aside Church business in order to provide for his family. The letter asked that the Saints assist in providing for him, and the response was impressive. About seventy men showed up at Joseph's home in Nauvoo to help out. One of the things the Prophet needed was wood, but he was not willing to just sit by and watch as everybody else did the work. Instead, he went out and cut down a white oak tree measuring five feet and four inches in diameter and hauled it to his property. The men then spent a pleasant day together sawing, splitting, and stacking a large amount of wood in the Prophet's yard.[20]

MIND AND SPIRIT

Some of the other enjoyments of Joseph Smith's life centered around mental and spiritual exercise. Some of his leisure time was spent in reading and meditation.[21] Sometimes he would challenge a friend to a game of checkers,[22] and on other occasions he would "play with the children in their games."[23]

Joseph would attend theatrical presentations in the evening in Nauvoo, watching such plays as *Damon and Pythias* and *The Idiot Witness*.[24]

The Prophet enjoyed posing riddles to those around him, and it was not uncommon to hear him matching couplets in rhyme.[25] A good example of this can be seen in his lengthy and insightful poetic rendition of the seventy-sixth section of the Doctrine and Covenants, which was published in the *Times and Seasons* newspaper in 1843.[26]

Historical sources reveal that the Prophet also loved to dance and "could sing well and loved music."[27] Among his favorite popular songs were "Wife, Children, and Friends," "The Battle of River Russen," "The Soldier's Tear," "The Soldier's Dream," and "The Last Rose of Summer."[28] Some of his favorite Church hymns included "When Joseph His Brethren Beheld," "Redeemer of Israel," and "The Spirit of God." Eunice Snow related that during the singing of these sacred songs "he would become so inspired with the spirit of the music that he would clap his hands and shout hosanna to the Lord."[29]

TRIALS

Joseph Smith's divine calling did not exempt him from the trials of life that are the common lot of humanity. And in many instances, his trials exceeded the threshold most mortals would care to endure.

LANGUAGE

One of Joseph's milder tribulations was a difficulty with language. Joseph acknowledged that he had some "imperfections" in his writing skills.[30] He complained of the "total darkness of paper, pen, and ink and a crooked, broken, scattered, and imperfect language." To him these were like a "little, narrow prison."[31] But he found a way to compensate for this difficulty by employing a number of scribes to assist him in the transaction of business.

In addition to his challenges with the written word, Joseph suffered from a "lack of fluency in address according to the *literati* of the age."[32] Peter Burnett, who was not a Latter-day Saint, thought that in conversation the Prophet was somewhat "slow, and used too many words to express his ideas, and would not generally go directly to the point."[33] Joseph also reportedly got nervous when it came time for him to speak in public. On this point Heber C. Kimball remarked, "I recollect often hearing brother Joseph Smith say that many times his legs trembled like Belshazzar's when he got up to speak before the world, and before the Saints" (cf. Dan. 5:6).[34]

One of Joseph Smith's favorite pieces of secular music was called "The Soldier's Tear" (text by Thomas H. Bayly and tune by George A. Lee). The words read,

> Upon the hill he turned,
> To take a last fond look
> Of the valley, and the village church,
> And the cottage by the brook.
> He listen'd to the sounds
> So familiar to his ear,
> And the soldier leant upon his sword,
> And wiped away a tear.
>
> Beside that cottage porch,
> A girl was on her knees;
> She held aloft a snowy scarf,
> Which fluttered in the breeze.
> She breath'd a prayer for him,
> A prayer he could not hear,
> But he paused to bless her as she knelt,
> And wiped away a tear.
>
> He turn'd, and left the spot,
> Oh! do not deem him weak,
> For dauntless was the soldier's heart,
> Tho' tears were on his cheek.
> Go watch the foremost ranks,
> In danger's dark career.
> Be sure the hand most daring there
> Has wiped away a tear.

See Thomas Haynes Bayly, *Songs, Ballads, and Other Poems* (London: Richard Bentley, 1844), 1:192—93.

THE NAUVOO BRASS BAND FLAG IS DECORATED with the All-Seeing Eye of God. Joseph Smith loved both secular and religious music. One source reports that he was also a good singer.

MOTIVATING THE SAINTS

Elder Kimball revealed that Joseph's trials also included a sense of frustration with some of the Latter-day Saints. He suffered a considerable degree of inner torment

> because this people would not live up to their privileges. There were many things he desired to reveal that we have not learned yet, but he could not do it. He said sometimes that he felt pressed upon . . . as though he were pent up in an acorn shell, and all because the people did not and would not prepare themselves to receive the rich treasures of wisdom and knowledge that he had to impart. He could have revealed a great many things to us if we had been ready; but he said there were many things that we could not receive because we lacked that diligence and faithfulness that were necessary to entitle us to those choice things of the kingdom.[35]

ILLNESS

Historical records indicate that the Prophet suffered from various illnesses during his lifetime, just like any other mortal. Some of these ailments were severe in their nature. As a child he contracted typhoid fever, a disease that eventually led to the removal of part of his lower left leg bone.[36] In 1834 he was overcome by cholera during the Zion's Camp march. The affliction to his body was excruciating, and he was only saved from death through the united prayers of himself, his brother Hyrum, and their mother.[37] In May 1832 he appears to have ingested some type of poison which caused him vomit so violently that he dislocated his jaw—which he replaced himself. The poison also caused much of his hair to fall out. He was healed of this illness in an instant when Newel K. Whitney blessed him in the name of the Lord by the laying on of hands.[38]

Joseph suffered from a severe illness in the summer of 1837 that nearly took his life. In response to this crisis, Brother Carter and several other Saints went into the Kirtland Temple, where they fasted and prayed for his recovery. Brother Carter "saw in a vision a grave open to receive him . . . but saw the earth fall in

SOMETIMES JOSEPH SMITH WAS FORCED TO DEAL with problems instigated by traitors and apostates. In this painting he and other Church leaders are taken prisoner at Far West, Missouri. The Prophet firmly believed that his capture at Far West and subsequent lengthy incarceration in Liberty Jail were brought about by a traitorous member of the Church (see Joseph Smith to Emma Smith, 4 November 1838, Community of Christ Archives, Independence, MO).

of its own accord and fill up the grave with no person in [it]." From this time forward the Prophet began a rapid recovery.[39]

Joseph, like many of the Saints, became sick during a malaria epidemic that struck Commerce, Illinois, during the summer of 1839, but he arose from his sickbed when "the power of God rested upon him. He commenced in his own house and . . . yard, commanding

the sick, in the name of Jesus Christ, to arise and be made whole, and they were healed according to his word. He then continued to travel from house to house [and] from tent to tent upon the bank of the river, healing the sick as he went."[40]

FINANCES

Another of Joseph Smith's earthly trials came in the form of financial difficulties. The Prophet grew up in a family that was poor, and he shared that fate for most of his life. Philo Dibble reported that Joseph was impoverished during the period of time he spent in Kirtland, Ohio.[41] This can be partly explained because of the great sacrifices that he made in order to construct the Kirtland Temple. On the other hand, a few of his monetary problems were brought about by sheer bad luck. In November 1836 he helped to set up a joint stock company called the Kirtland Safety Society. A year later the United States went through a substantial financial panic, and many banks around the country closed, including the Kirtland institution. Joseph was left in deep debt.[42]

Some of Joseph's financial difficulties were forced upon him. In Far West, Missouri, for instance, he "contracted [debt] through . . . persecution . . . and vexatious lawsuits."[43] By October 1841 his earthly possessions amounted to a horse and an old cow that were given to him as gifts, two pet deer, six turkeys, his dog, and a little household furniture.[44]

JOSEPH SMITH WAS ONE OF THE FOUNDERS of the Kirtland Safety Society. He was associated with this financial institution from November 1836 until June 1837. He even served as one of its chief officers, as evidenced by his signature on this five-dollar note. But a troubled national economy and the apparent embezzlement of large sums of money brought about the institution's downfall—and plunged the Prophet into deep debt.

TRIALS OF FAITH

Even with all of the marvelous spiritual manifestations granted to Joseph Smith, he still experienced trials of faith. Heber C. Kimball provided an example in this category. "I have heard Joseph say many times, that he was much tempted about the revelations the Lord gave through him—it seemed to be so impossible for them to be fulfilled."[45] Brigham Young said that "Joseph had to pray all the time, exercise faith, live his religion, and magnify his calling [in order] to obtain the manifestations of the Lord, and to keep him steadfast in the faith."[46]

PERSECUTION

Harassment from Joseph's persecutors also tested his faith. Joseph was warned by the angel Moroni in September 1823 that his name would be had not only for good but also for evil among all the nations of the earth.[47] And it did not take long for this prophecy to find fulfillment. The Prophet was endlessly vilified both in the public press and in private circles, being called such things as a deceiver, a fanatic, a money-monger, a scoundrel, an egotist, a hypocrite, and a fool.

The harassment was not limited to words. Katherine Smith reported that after word began to circulate in Palmyra, New York, about the restoration of the gospel through Joseph Smith, people would throw rocks and sticks at his house.[48] One time a mob—at the instigation of Christian ministers, no less—tore apart a temporary font where Joseph was trying to baptize a few converts. When he and others rebuilt the structure the next day, the mob returned; this time they were "raging with anger" and seemed determined to commit acts of violence against the assembled Saints.[49]

Sometimes Joseph even suffered physical abuse at the hands of his enemies. In 1827, when he attempted to bring the golden plates of the Book of Mormon out of a hiding place and into his family's home, he was beaten with guns by three individuals. He also dislocated his thumb when he struck his third attacker.[50]

During one of about forty-seven lawsuits that were brought against the Prophet, he was incarcerated, was not allowed to eat any food, and, in a scene reminiscent of the life of the Savior, was insulted and spat upon. His tormenters then pointed their fingers at him and,

THE ANGEL MORONI PROPHESIED IN 1823 THAT Joseph Smith's reputation as a man would be vilified and he would be heavily persecuted because of his mission and message (see *Messenger and Advocate,* vol. 2, no. 13, October 1835, 200). This painting by C. C. A. Christensen depicts a mob preparing to tar and feather the Prophet in Hiram, Ohio, in 1832. Sidney Rigdon, who was also attacked by this group of ruffians, can be seen lying unconscious on the ground.

in ridiculing tones, called out, "Prophesy! Prophesy!" (cf. Matt. 26:67–68).[51]

But this was only a precursor of cruel things to come. While residing in Hiram, Ohio, in 1832, Joseph was pulled out of bed one night by a drunken mob (which included Christians from various denominations) and dragged into the wintry air. Once outside, these men swore at Joseph, choked him, scratched him, tore his hair out, attempted to pour nitric acid down his throat, broke out one of his teeth, and covered him in tar and feathers. During this mob action one of Joseph's adopted twins contracted a severe cold, possibly from exposure to the elements. The young child died shortly thereafter.[52]

Near the end of his life Joseph was kidnapped in front of his wife. His abductors then proceeded to jab him in the ribcage so hard and so many times with their pistols that his skin bruised till it turned black.[53]

Though Joseph's trials tested his faith, he firmly trusted in the Lord. Said he, "As for the perils which I am called to pass through, they seem but a small thing to me, as the envy and wrath of man have been my common lot all the days of my life; . . . deep water is what I am [accustomed] to swim in. It has become a second nature to me; and I feel, like Paul [the apostle], to glory in tribulation" (D&C 127:2). "I hope for the best always in all circumstances. Although I go unto death, I will trust in God. . . . [I] can only pray for deliverance, until it is meted out, and take everything as it comes, with patience and fortitude."[54] "For my part, I think I never could have felt as I now do, if I had not suffered the wrongs that I have suffered. All things shall work together for the good of them that love God."[55]

CHAPTER 5

A Disciple in THOUGHT, WORD, & DEED

JOSEPH SMITH HAD BEEN TAUGHT TO ACCEPT AND REVERE JESUS CHRIST FROM THE TIME HE WAS A SMALL CHILD. In the spring of 1820 he unexpectedly found himself in the hallowed presence of his Redeemer. From the mouth of God the Father, who was also standing above him in the air, he was told, "This is my Beloved Son. Hear Him!" (JS–H 1:17). Joseph heard the words of his Master.during this marvelous manifestation. Throughout his life he strove to emulate the Son of God in thought, word, and deed.

THE

BOOK OF MORMON:

AN ACCOUNT WRITTEN BY THE HAND OF MOR-MON, UPON PLATES TAKEN FROM THE PLATES OF NEPHI.

Wherefore it is an abridgment of the Record of the People of Nephi; and also of the Lamanites; written to the Lamanites, which are a remnant of the House of Israel; and also to Jew and Gentile; written by way of commandment, and also by the spirit of Prophesy and of Revelation. Written, and sealed up, and hid up unto the LORD, that they might not be destroyed, to come forth by the gift and power of GOD, unto the interpretation thereof; sealed by the hand of Moroni, and hid up unto the LORD, to come forth in due time by the way of Gentile; the interpretation thereof by the gift of GOD; an abridgment taken from the Book of Ether.

Also, which is a Record of the People of Jared, which were scattered at the time the LORD confounded the language of the people when they were building a tower to get to Heaven: which is to shew unto the remnant of the House of Israel how great things the LORD hath done for their fathers; and that they may know the covenants of the LORD, that they are not cast off forever; and also to the convincing of the Jew and Gentile that JESUS is the CHRIST, the ETERNAL GOD, manifesting Himself unto all nations. And now if there be fault, it be the mistake of men; wherefore condemn not the things of GOD, that ye may be found spotless at the judgment seat of CHRIST.

BY JOSEPH SMITH, JUNIOR,
AUTHOR AND PROPRIETOR.

PALMYRA:

PRINTED BY E. B. GRANDIN, FOR THE AUTHOR.

1830.

THE PURPOSE OF the Book of Mormon, as explicitly stated on the title page of this 1830 first edition, is to convince both "Jew and Gentile that Jesus is the Christ, the Eternal God, manifesting Himself unto all nations." It is also designed to bring individuals who belong to the house of Israel to a knowledge of "the covenants of the Lord."

THOUGHT

The private writings of Joseph Smith, such as his journal entries and letters, serve as a window into his thoughts, offering glimpses of his inner devotion to Christ. Some writings are brief yet significant, such as the letter written to William W. Phelps wherein the

Christ's sake and for no other cause." Yet he reassured her with these words: "[W]e are in good spirits and rejoice that we are counted worthy to be persecuted for Christ's sake."[4]

One of the more striking entries in Joseph's journal is a prayer to God the Father for increased faith on the name of His Son. The motivation behind this request speaks volumes about the heart of Joseph Smith. He

THIS FOURTEEN-BY-FOUR-INCH HAND-PAINTED SIGN MARKED THE LOCATION OF THE OFFICE OF PRESIDENT Joseph Smith. It was created sometime after April 1838, when the current name of the Church was revealed (see D&C 115:3–4). It is known that President Smith conducted Church business in his Nauvoo homestead office from the spring of 1840 to January 1842 and thereafter in an office on the upper level of his Red Brick Store. Notice the pronounced emphasis on Jesus Christ in the name of the Church.

Prophet affirmed that he was the servant of Jehovah.[1] In a correspondence with Oliver Cowdery dated 22 October 1829, the Prophet expressed his desire that God preserve both of them in a spotless condition (since they had recently received the ordinance of baptism) and then eventually receive all of the Saints "to rest with Him in eternal repose through the atonement of Christ our Lord."[2]

Joseph desired that glory and honor be given to Jesus Christ. This sentiment is evidenced by a journal entry made during one of his proselytizing missions. On the pages of the journal, he petitioned, "May God carry on His work in this place till all shall know Him . . . [and] may God increase the gifts [of the Spirit] among them for His Son's sake."[3] And Joseph was willing to suffer for the Son's sake as well. In 1838 he was betrayed by false brethren at Far West, Missouri, and subsequently confined in a squalid dungeon. On 12 November 1838 he wrote to Emma, saying, "[W]e are prisoners in chains, and under strong guards, for

desired to be able to receive not only more revelation but also a stronger determination to live according to God's holy laws. This entry reads,

> O, Thou who seeth, and knoweth the hearts of all men; . . . that sitteth . . . enthroned in heaven; look down upon thy servant Joseph, at this time; and let faith on the name of thy Son Jesus Christ, to a greater degree than Thy servant ever yet has enjoyed, be conferred upon him; even the faith of Elijah; and let the lamp of eternal life be lit up in his heart, never to be taken away; and let the words of eternal life, be poured upon the soul of thy servant; that he may know Thy will, Thy statutes, and Thy commandments, and Thy judgments to do them.[5]

Joseph's undeviating devotion to the Savior can be seen in another letter that he wrote to Emma in the year 1832. In this communication he expressed his delight at finding her "still in the faith of Christ." He told her, "God is my friend. In him I shall find comfort. I have given my life into His hands. I am prepared to go at His call." He then wrote a few words that reveal the depth and breadth of his commitment to the Son of God: "I desire to be with Christ. I count not my life dear to me only to do His will."[6]

Curtis E. Bolton:

I testify that I personally knew Joseph Smith.
I have lived with him in his family;
was with him morning, noon, and night,
early and late. I saw him in most trying
situations, with friends and enemies;
and in all the time that I remained
in his family, I never saw the slightest act,
nor heard one word,
unbecoming a man of God.

John Taylor, *Three Nights' Public Discussion*
(Liverpool, England: John Taylor, 1850), 24.

WORD

Joseph Smith's public teachings about Jesus Christ are among the most visible marks of his discipleship, and they serve to establish his credentials as a true prophet of God. His basic message to humanity was that he "professed to be nothing but a man, and a minister of salvation, sent by Jesus Christ to preach the gospel."[7]

At the request of a Chicago newspaper editor named John Wentworth, the Prophet prepared a brief summary of Church beliefs to be published before the world; this list, prepared in 1842, eventually became known as the Articles of Faith. The centrality of Jesus Christ is readily apparent to even a casual reader. Among the Articles of Faith are statements such as these: "We believe in . . . Jesus Christ"; "We believe that through the Atonement of Christ, all mankind may be saved"; "We believe that the first principles . . . of the gospel are: first, Faith in the Lord Jesus Christ";

"We believe . . . that Christ will reign personally upon the earth" during the Millennium (A of F 1, 3, 4, 10).[8]

"The fundamental principles of our religion," said Joseph on another occasion, "are the testimony of the apostles and prophets, concerning Jesus Christ, that He died, was buried, and rose again the third day, and ascended unto heaven; and all other things which pertain to our religion are only appendages to it."[9]

Brigham Young provided some of the specific details of Joseph's Smith's Christology. He said during one of his public sermons,

Joseph told us that Jesus was the Christ, the Mediator between God and man, and the Savior of the world. He told us that there was no other name in the heavens nor under the heavens, neither could there be, by which mankind could be saved in the presence of the Father, but by and through the name and ministry of Jesus Christ, and the atonement He made on Mount Calvary. Joseph also told us that the Savior requires strict obedience to all the commandments, ordinances, and laws pertaining to His kingdom, and that if we would do this we should be made partakers of all the blessings promised in His gospel.[10]

Joseph Smith declared that the objective of the church restored through his instrumentality was to "preach the gospel in all humility and meekness, and warn sinners to repent and come to Christ."[11] On a more personal level, he clearly understood that in conjunction with his calling he had a responsibility to teach the Saints "the principles of righteousness, and lead them agreeably to the will of heaven; so that they may be perfected, and prepared to meet the Lord Jesus Christ" either in this world or in the world to come.[12]

The Prophet also understood that a person who champions the cause of righteousness on this fallen earth will be met with intense opposition. "He that will war the true Christian warfare against the corruptions of these last days," he said, "will have wicked men and angels of devils, and all the infernal powers of darkness continually arrayed against him." Nevertheless, "when wicked and corrupt men oppose, it is a criterion to judge if a man is warring the Christian warfare." For a proof text, Joseph referred to Matthew 5:11, wherein the Savior says, "Blessed are ye, when men shall revile you, and persecute you, and shall say all manner of evil against you falsely, for my sake."[13] And Joseph was willing, and taught others, to suffer persecution in faithfulness to the end. He said that "a good man will endure all things to honor Christ, and even dispose of the whole world, and all in it, to save his soul."[14]

DEED

Living the teachings of the Lord and following His divine example are unmistakable signs of discipleship. Joseph Smith taught the Latter-day Saints that this was the course they were to take; they were to "copy from the Savior, who is our pattern."[15] It is evident from an examination of the deeds of Joseph Smith that he was not just a preacher of the word, but a doer also—a sincere and dedicated disciple of Christ.

The Lord said, "For I was an hungred, and ye gave me meat: I was thirsty, and ye gave me drink: I was a stranger, and ye took me in: Naked, and ye clothed me: I was sick, and ye visited me: I was in prison, and ye came unto me. . . . Verily I say unto you, Inasmuch as ye have done it unto one of the least of these my brethren, ye have done it unto me" (Matt. 25:35–36, 40). There are incidents in the life of Joseph Smith that reflect the actions named by the Savior in this passage of scripture. A few of many recorded examples follow.

For I was an hungred, and ye gave me meat. When the Nightingale and Leech families emigrated from Great Britain to Nauvoo, Illinois, in 1841, they had difficulty finding employment, and after about six weeks their provisions were running low. Henry Nightingale and James Leech decided to approach the Prophet to see if he had some kind of work for them to do. Henry was reluctant,

THE SAINTS OFTEN MET TO HEAR THE PROPHET preach the doctrines of Christ in the shaded groves of Nauvoo, Illinois. On 20 March 1842 in the grove that stood just to the west of the temple, Joseph spoke on the redemption of little children through "the blood of the Lamb" (*WJS,* 109). This modern replica of an open-air chapel has been constructed to the southwest of the new Nauvoo Temple site.

because he was not a convert, but they made their petition to Joseph at his Red Brick Store down by the river. After questioning them about their skills, the Prophet asked if they would dig a ditch for him three feet wide and two and a half feet deep. They agreed. The Prophet marked out the spot, and they went about their labor.

After a time the work was completed, and Joseph insisted that the two men go into his store and pick out the best pieces of ham that they could find. They protested that they had not done enough work for so generous a payment, but the Prophet said he was satisfied with their effort. He selected the best of the pork for the two men, loaded them with two sacks of flour, and sent them on their way.[16]

I was a stranger, and ye took me in. On a winter night in 1843 a fourteen-year-old boy arrived in Nauvoo looking for his brother. The boy was informed that his brother lived eight miles distant, and because of the darkness and snowy ground, he was advised to go to the Mansion House and stay there for the evening. When the boy arrived, Joseph Smith welcomed him and said, "Come in, son, we'll take care of you." The boy was warmed by the fire, given some food, and supplied with a room. The next day brought a bitter chill, and Joseph told the boy that he should stay there until some teams drove into town and then he could be taken out to see his brother. The boy informed the Prophet that he had no money to pay for his accommodations, but he was told not to concern himself about that; he would be taken care of regardless of his circumstances.[17]

Naked, and ye clothed me. In 1836 the Lord issued a call through the Prophet Joseph Smith for Elder John E. Page, a member of the Twelve, to go on a mission to the Canadian provinces. The Apostle objected, because he was at that time "destitute of clothing." Upon hearing this, Joseph took his own coat from his back, handed it to Elder Page, and told him to go on his mission and "the Lord would bless him abundantly."[18]

JOSEPH SMITH FOLLOWED THE SAVIOR'S ADMONITION to feed the hungry. This photograph shows the kitchen in Joseph's Mansion House in Nauvoo. The green chairs at the kitchen table belonged to Joseph and Emma Smith and were part of the Mansion House's original furniture.

Joseph Smith proclaimed his determination to defend the religious rights of all men and women, regardless of their affiliation. He said,

If it has been demonstrated that I have been willing to die for a "Mormon," I am bold to declare before heaven that I am just as ready to die in defending the rights of a Presbyterian, a Baptist, or a good man of any other denomination; for the same principle which would trample upon the rights of the Latter-day Saints would trample upon the rights of the Roman Catholics, or of any other denomination who may be unpopular and too weak to defend themselves.

HC, 5:498.

Jane Manning James told another story about the Prophet's kindheartedness. Jane (a freeborn black woman from Wilton, Connecticut) and eight other members of her extended family walked across the country to Nauvoo, Illinois, in the fall of 1843. She related,

When I [came to Nauvoo] I only had two things on me, no shoes nor stockings, wore them all out on the road. I had a trunk full of beautiful clothes, which I had sent around by water, and I was thinking of having them when I got to Nauvoo, and they stole them at St. Louis, and I did not have a rag of them. . . . One morning, before [Joseph Smith] came in, I had been up to the landing and found all my clothes were gone. Well, I sat there crying. He came in and looked around. . . . To Sister Emma, he said, "go and clothe her up, go down to the store and clothe her up." Sister Emma

THE NAUVOO HOMESTEAD, LOOKING SOUTH toward the Mississippi River. The light-colored log structure on the far left of this complex is the portion that the Prophet purchased when he first moved to Nauvoo in 1839. Joseph Smith exemplified the teachings of the Redeemer when he gave up this home for the care of the sick and afflicted.

HOLINESS
TO THE
LORD
·
THE HOUSE
OF THE
LORD

did. She got me clothes by the bolt. I had everything.[19]

I was sick, and ye visited me. The Prophet personally cared for both his father and his mother when they were ill. Not only did he give them nourishment and attend to things that needed to be done around their house, but he also provided transportation to the countryside in order to promote their recuperation.[20]

There are numerous accounts of Joseph Smith bestowing blessings upon the sick and afflicted. John Harper, for example, reported that in late December 1843 he had a violent pain in his right side. After he had endured the pain for two days, his wife urged him to go and seek a priesthood blessing. John took a cane and, with its assistance, walked down to the Mansion House, where he inquired if the Prophet was in the building. Joseph was summoned from the upper floor; he went to the side of this ailing man and asked him to take a chair. Brother Harper related that at this point, "he laid his hands on my head and rebuked the pain in the name of the Lord and when he took his hands off my head I was healed and went home rejoicing in the name of the God of my salvation and have never been troubled with it since that time."[21]

Wandle Mace reported that in 1839, when so many of the Saints were suffering from malaria and other diseases in Commerce, Illinois, and Montrose, Iowa, "Joseph gave his house up to the sick, and moved his family into a large tent." But that was not all. He and his wife "took care of them, [and] they extended their labors as far as possible. Joseph and Emma would ride on horseback, from place to place visiting the sick . . . and reliev[ing] their wants."[22]

I was in prison, and ye came unto me. Mary F. Adams told of an incident that occurred while Joseph was acting as the mayor of Nauvoo (sometime after 19 May 1842). A black man by the name of Anthony had been arrested for violating the law against selling liquor, and he was subsequently brought before the mayor. Anthony explained to Joseph that he had engaged in this illegal activity because he had previously purchased his own freedom and that of his wife, and now he wished to purchase the freedom of his child. Joseph said, "I am sorry, Anthony, but the law must be observed, and we will have to impose a fine." But the next day Joseph gave Anthony one of his own fine horses, insisting that he sell it and use the funds to purchase the child's freedom.[23]

As part of his foreordained mission, Joseph Smith was instrumental in freeing millions of prisoners who resided or would reside in the spiritual realm. On 21 January 1836 the Lord showed Joseph a vision of the future and taught him concepts related to salvation for the dead. Joseph learned that his deceased brother Alvin qualified for an inheritance in the celestial kingdom of God, even though he had not been baptized by a legitimate priesthood representative before he died (see D&C 137). On 14 August 1840 the Prophet publicly announced that baptisms for the dead would be practiced in conjunction with the Nauvoo Temple, and several years later he taught the Saints that "all those [who] die in the faith go to the prison of spirits to preach to the dead in body, but they are alive in the spirit, and those spirits preach to the spirits that they may live according to God in the spirit, and men do minister for them in the flesh" through vicarious ordinances.[24]

Joseph Smith was a genuine disciple of Jesus Christ, and his discipleship was manifest in his thoughts, his words, and his deeds. As a result of his Christlike life, he was a fit companion for the Holy Ghost, that spiritual Being who testifies of the divinity of the Son (see John 15:26). William Henrie observed that "you could not be in [the Prophet's] presence without feeling the influence and Spirit of God, which seemed to flow from him almost as heat does from a stove. You could not see it, but you felt it."[25]

THE DEDICATION PLAQUE ON THE EAST SIDE OF the new Nauvoo Temple proclaiming it to be a "House of the Lord." Joseph Smith was the instrument through which God restored temple ordinances to the earth. These sacred rites are designed to help those who have come unto Christ to become like Him in the fullest sense possible.

"THIS IS MY BELOVED SON, HEAR HIM!"

CHAPTER 6

Restoring GOD'S KINGDOM

JOSEPH SMITH WAS CHOSEN AS THE INSTRUMENT THROUGH WHICH GOD WOULD RESTORE HIS KINGDOM TO THE EARTH IN THE LATTER DAYS. The Prophet's calling was no random act, however. This solemn assignment was given to him in the courts of the premortal realm. When the appointed time arrived for him to carry out his earthly task, he was not simply reminded of his duties and then left to himself; rather, he was assisted on a continual basis by heavenly messengers and the revelations of the Lord.

PREMORTAL ASSIGNMENT

Joseph Smith was not chosen arbitrarily to restore God's kingdom to the earth during the final dispensation of the gospel, and scriptural records and the teachings of early LDS Church leaders bear this out. The Lord knew Jeremiah in premortal times and ordained him to be a prophet before he was born on the earth (see Jer. 1:5). It was no different with the Prophet Joseph Smith. When President Joseph F. Smith (the son of Hyrum Smith) was shown a vision of the premortal life on 3 October 1918, he learned that Joseph Smith was "among the noble and great ones who were chosen in the beginning to be rulers in the Church of God. Even before they were born, they, with many others, received their first lessons in the world of spirits and were prepared to come forth in the due time of the Lord to labor in His vineyard for the

---

THIS STAINED-GLASS WINDOW DEPICTS JOSEPH SMITH'S FIRST VISION, WHICH occurred in the spring of 1820. In one recital of this sacred event, the Prophet related that he saw not only the Father and the Son but also many angels.

salvation of the souls of men" (D&C 138:55–56). Many years before this vision took place, President Brigham Young taught,

> It was decreed in the councils of eternity, long before the foundations of the earth were laid, that [Joseph Smith] should be the man, in the last dispensation of this world, to bring forth the word of God to the people, and receive the fullness of the keys and power of the Priesthood of the Son of God. The Lord had His eye upon him, and upon his father, and upon his father's father, and upon their progenitors clear back to Abraham, and from Abraham to the flood, from the flood to Enoch, and from Enoch to Adam. He has watched that family and that blood as it has circulated from its fountain to the birth of that man. [Joseph Smith] was foreordained in eternity to preside over this last dispensation.[1]

It is evident that the Prophet learned of his foreordination as he translated ancient scriptural texts. As he brought forth the Book of Mormon and restored parts of the Old Testament, he read of a choice seer whom the Lord prophesied would be raised up in the last days—a seer who would bring forth the word of the Lord, who would have enemies seeking his destruction,

and who would be named Joseph (see 2 Ne. 3:6–18; JST, Gen. 50:26–33).

Over time the Prophet may have learned more details concerning his premortal identity and calling. On 29 June 1844 William W. Phelps declared that Joseph Smith had "royal kindred" in the spirit world from whom he received "the keys, the power, and the mystery" of the gospel. Phelps claimed that the Prophet was "one of the holy ones commissioned by his Father among the royal Seventy, when the high council of heaven set them apart to come down" upon the earth. "Joseph Smith . . . was [called] Gazelam in the spirit world," according to Brother Phelps (cf. Alma 37:23).[2] In what appears to be a direct statement regarding his premortal identity, Joseph Smith once publicly exclaimed, "Would to God, brethren, I could tell you who I am!"[3]

In light of the preceding information, it is not surprising that Asael Smith, Joseph's paternal grandfather, had a premonition that one of his descendants would "promulgate a work to revolutionize the world of religious faith."[4] He eventually became convinced that Joseph Smith Jr., his grandson, "was the very prophet that he had long known would come in his family."[5]

MORTAL CALLING

Joseph Smith taught that "the kingdom of God was set upon the earth in all ages from the days of Adam to the present time whenever there was a man on earth who had authority to administer the ordinances of the gospel or a priest of God and unto such a man God did reveal His will."[6] Each of the ancient dispensations ended with a falling away from the truth and a loss of authority.

When Jesus Christ lived on the earth, He established a new dispensation of the gospel. He bestowed "the keys of the kingdom" upon Peter (Matt. 16:19) so

THIS PORTION OF THE PRINTER'S MANUSCRIPT OF the Book of Mormon displays a prophecy found in 2 Nephi 3:5–7. The prophecy, which speaks of the Lord raising up a choice seer in the latter days, refers to the Prophet Joseph Smith.

THE RAYS OF THE MORNING SUN SHINE THROUGH the trees of the Sacred Grove in Palmyra, New York. Seth Chapman, who professed to be one of Joseph Smith's boyhood friends, said that the Prophet told him the First Vision occurred in the wooded area on the west end of the family farm (see *Ensign*, April 1990, 16).

that the chief Apostle could direct the affairs of the kingdom after His Ascension into heaven. But after Peter's death the pure doctrines and ordinances of the gospel became corrupted, as in all previous dispensations. Legitimate priesthood authority to administer the kingdom was also eventually lost from the earth.

In the early part of the nineteenth century, Joseph Smith began to notice the confusion and strife that had resulted from the Apostasy of the previous dispensation. In 1820 his desire for personal salvation and understanding led him to a secluded grove of trees on his family farm, where he humbly petitioned the Lord for clarification. The initial response was a desperate assault by the powers of darkness to prevent the reestablishment of the Lord's kingdom on the earth. But the Father drove the adversary from the grove, and in a pillar of light He descended with His Beloved Son. Joseph was informed by these divine Beings that "all religious denominations were believing in incorrect doctrines, and that none of them was acknowledged of God as His Church and kingdom: and [he] was expressly commanded 'to go not after them,' at the same time receiving a promise that the fullness of the gospel should at some future time be made known unto [him]."[7]

The keys of "the kingdom of God on the earth" (D&C 97:14) were eventually bestowed upon Joseph Smith and other Church leaders (D&C 81:1–2; 115:19; see also 42:69; 64:4; 65:2, 5–6). This latter-day kingdom was unique, however, in that it was not to suffer the same fate as the ones established in previous dispensations, for it was to be the last (see D&C 90:2, 6), and the keys of this kingdom were to be returned to Jesus Christ when He came to rule and reign personally upon the earth during the Millennium (see D&C 112:15–16).

Joseph Smith testified that he was in reality called and authorized by God the Father "to lay the foundation of this great work and kingdom in this dispensation."[8] This, declared Joseph, is the kingdom foretold by the biblical prophet Daniel (see Dan. 2:44–45).[9] And this is

THE ANGEL MORONI TURNS OVER CUSTODY OF THE Book of Mormon plates to Joseph Smith Jr. (22 September 1827) in this painting by Gary E. Smith. As the Prophet translated this record, he learned about the form and function of the kingdom of God in ancient days and was thereby assisted in fulfilling his mission of restoring the kingdom to the earth.

"a day in which the God of heaven has begun to restore the ancient order of His kingdom unto His servants and His people, a day in which all things are concurring to bring about the completion of the fullness of the gospel, a fullness of the dispensation of dispensations, even the fullness of times."[10] Not surprisingly, Joseph's greatest motto in life was "God and His Kingdom."[11]

THE WORK OF RESTORATION

The Lord restored His kingdom to the earth by providing Joseph Smith with a succession of visions, visitations, and revelations.[12] On 22 September 1823 an angel named Moroni was sent to the Prophet in fulfillment of a prophecy uttered two thousand years before by John the Revelator (see Rev. 14:6).[13] The angel's duty was to inform Joseph of an ancient record preserved by God's covenant people who lived in the Americas. Joseph was given the assignment to translate this record—called the Book of Mormon—and then utilize its contents in the formal organization of the Church of Jesus Christ in April 1830.[14]

Divine authority, or priesthood, was also necessary in the restoration of God's kingdom to the earth. In order to bestow this necessary power, the Lord sent several messengers from the previous gospel dispensation. John the Baptist (a direct descendant of Aaron, the chief temple priest) came and bestowed the Aaronic Priesthood on Joseph Smith and Oliver Cowdery. The two mortal men were visited shortly thereafter by Peter, James, and John, the Savior's meridian Apostles, who bestowed the higher priesthood named after Melchizedek. The priesthood of Aaron was to focus its energies on temporal matters, while the Melchizedek Priesthood was to focus on things of a spiritual nature. Both of these priesthoods were restored in 1829.

Once Joseph Smith obtained a correct knowledge of the form and function of gospel ordinances, he was able to administer them so that they would be acknowledged by the Lord both in time and in eternity. These ordinances included blessing children at birth, baptism at the age of accountability, the laying on of hands for the gift of the Holy Ghost, ordination to administrative office, the blessing of the sick and afflicted, and the numerous rites of the temple. Some of the keys pertaining to the fullness of temple work were restored to Joseph Smith and Oliver Cowdery inside the Kirtland Temple in 1836. Moses, Elias, and Elijah were sent to perform these labors, and their visitations are noted in section 110 of the Doctrine and Covenants. The temple ordinances restored through the Prophet were the very same ordinances performed by the ancient Israelites and early Christians.[15] The purpose of these rites is to eventually bring about the exaltation of those individuals who have entered into God's

THIS PAGE FROM THE 1835 edition of the LDS hymnal shows song no. 26, "Now We'll Sing with One Accord" (words by William W. Phelps). Originally written in present tense, the text refers to the Great Apostasy, the restoration of the priesthood through angelic means, the translation of the Book of Mormon, and the Savior's command to Joseph Smith to go and prune His vineyard.

1 Now we'll sing with one accord,
For a prophet of the Lord,
Bringing forth his precious word,
    Cheers the saints as anciently.

2 When the world in darkness lay,
Lo, he sought the better way,
And he heard the Savior say,
    "Go and prune my vineyard, son!"

3 And an angel surely, then,
For a blessing unto men,
Brought the priesthood back again,
    In its ancient purity.

4 Even Joseph he inspires;
Yea, his heart he truly fires,
With the light that he desires
    For the work of righteousness.

5 And the book of Mormon, true,
With its cov'nant ever new,
For the Gentile and the Jew,
    He translated sacredly.

6 The commandments to the church,
Which the saints will always search,

B

kingdom. Joseph Smith, under divine direction, also inaugurated proxy temple work for those who have died but who are eligible to receive all of the blessings that are available in the kingdom of God.[16]

Between the ages of twenty-four and thirty-seven, Joseph Smith brought forth an impressive amount of scriptural material. He even described such activity as a branch of his calling.[17] The Book of Mormon is 531

> Stephen S. Harding, who served as one of the governors of the Utah Territory, was present in Egbert B. Grandin's printing shop in 1829 "when the proof sheet of the first form of the [Book of Mormon], including the title page," was struck off. After some revision had been done a "corrected impression" was made and "it was passed around to the young prophet" and some other believers who were present. Harding noted that they all "appeared to be delighted with the dawning of the new gospel dispensation."
>
> Pomeroy Tucker, *Origin, Rise, and Progress of Mormonism* (New York: D. Appleton and Co., 1867), 284–85.

pages long. Doctrine and Covenants sections 1 through 134, sections brought forth by Joseph Smith, number 280 pages. The material in the Pearl of Great Price is 58 pages in length, and there are approximately 30 pages worth of writings from the Joseph Smith Translation of the Old and New Testaments, bringing the total number of pages of scripture brought forth by the Prophet to almost 900.[18] Among the ancient records that Joseph restored to the latter-day dispensation are writings by prophets like Adam, Enoch, Moses, Abraham, and Joseph of Egypt.[19] And, of course, Joseph Smith spent fourteen years expounding upon these scriptures from the pulpit and in private circles—leaving behind hundreds of pages of valuable commentary and insight.

One of Joseph Smith's most important tasks as the inaugural prophet of the dispensation of the fullness of times was to provide mankind with untainted doctrine.

Among the many truths restored through the Prophet, the most important are probably those pertaining to the Godhead, mankind, the Creation, and the plan of salvation.

Joseph knew from personal experience that the confusing creeds of Christendom are incorrect in their notions about Deity. Joseph taught the simple truth that the Father, Son, and Holy Ghost are three individual personages; the first two are resurrected beings and the third a spirit who will someday receive a body like the others.[20] Instead of an ethereal substance without body, parts, or passions, God "was once as we are now, and is an exalted man."[21]

Joseph also taught that men and women are, in the most literal sense, the children of God created in His image. Jesus Christ was the firstborn child of the Father, but all of God's children have the potential to progress and eventually become like their divine Parent, just as the Firstborn Son actually did (see D&C 76:50–70; 131:1–4; 132:19–20).

Joseph Smith restored the knowledge that God has created "worlds without number" (Moses 1:33). But they were not created out of nothing, as some Christian sects teach, but rather out of existing matter. Said the Prophet, "This earth was organized or formed out of other planets which were broke[n] up and remodeled and made into the one on which we live."[22] In addition, Joseph learned that the creation of the earth was accomplished by the delegation of God's authority to other divine beings (see Moses 2:1; Abr. 4:1).

As Joseph Smith was schooled in the doctrines of the Restoration, he became familiar with the details of the great plan of salvation. He learned that existence consists of a premortal period of growth and decision, a mortal probation with various tests and opportunities, and then multiple postmortal rewards of darkness or glory to be assigned after divine judgment. He became aware that husbands and wives could be sealed together on earth by the power of the holy priesthood, and if they stayed faithful to their covenants, they would remain together throughout all eternity and progress to become like their Progenitor. Joseph was also informed about the condition of those who die without a knowledge of Christ's gospel and the opportunities that are made available to them for their personal salvation (see D&C 137:5–10).

In addition to these other works of restoration, Joseph Smith did three very important things in connection with God's earthly kingdom shortly before his death. First, on 11 March 1844 he organized a group called the Council of Fifty. This council, which included several people who were not Latter-day Saints, was a prototype of the worldwide government that would function after the Second Coming of Christ.[23] Second, Joseph Smith was ordained as the king of the Council of Fifty. Just as a king ruled in ancient Israel as a representative of the heavenly King, so it was to be among the restored house of Israel during the latter days and Millennium—a kingdom must be ruled by a king.[24] And third, Joseph Smith sealed all of the keys of the kingdom that he had received from God upon the heads of the Twelve Apostles. Wilford Woodruff, in recalling this incident, said,

> [U]pon our shoulders he rolled the burden of the kingdom, and he gave us all the keys and powers and gifts to carry on this great and mighty work. He told us that he had received every key, every power and every gift for the salvation of the living and the dead, and he said: "Upon the Twelve I seal these gifts and powers and keys from henceforth and forever. No matter what may come to me. And I lay this work upon your shoulders. Take it and bear it off, and if you don't, you'll be damned."[25]

By taking this action Joseph ensured that the keys would not be lost from the earth and the kingdom would continue to prosper after his death. Like the prophecy of Daniel proclaims, the latter-day kingdom, which was restored through Joseph Smith, will never be thrown down but continue to grow until it fills the whole earth.

(OPPOSITE) EXALTATION IS THE GREATEST GIFT THAT God can bestow upon those who unite themselves with His kingdom and serve Him in righteousness unto the end. Latter-day Saints enter into several covenants that pertain to exaltation at temple altars like this one from the house of the Lord in Manti, Utah.

THIS PAIR OF CLASPED MALE AND FEMALE HANDS IS chiseled into a headstone that is located in the Old Nauvoo City cemetery. Above the hands can be seen the weather-worn phrase, "WE PART TO MEET AGAIN," reflecting the ancient doctrine (restored through the Prophet Joseph Smith) of marriage for time and all eternity.

THIS WOODEN CANE, WHICH BELONGED TO THE Prophet Joseph Smith, is carved with his initials. A crown, indicative of royal status, can be seen above the shield on which the initials are displayed.

CHAPTER 7

PUBLIC
Professions

GIVEN JOSEPH SMITH'S TIME-CONSUMING OCCUPATION AS AN ECCLESIASTICAL LEADER, IT IS SOMEWHAT SURPRISING THAT HE ALSO PLAYED A VARIETY OF ROLES IN THE CIVIC AFFAIRS OF HIS DAY. Joseph greatly cherished his citizenship in the United States of America,[1] and so it was natural for him to desire to make public contributions in his community.

During his lifetime the Prophet served in a wide range of secular capacities, including chief magistrate, registrar of deeds, architect, chairman of at least five municipal committees, farmer, partner in the United Firm, attorney, day-laborer, bank officer, city councilman, member of an agricultural and mechanical association, vice-mayor, and mayor. A few of the Prophet's other public positions, briefly explored on the following pages, show a rounded view of his life.

CITY PLANNER

Joseph Smith began his work as a city planner by divine directive. The Lord indicated in a number of revelations that a New Jerusalem would be built upon the American continent in the latter days and was to be called the City of Zion (see D&C 28:9; 45:65–67) or Mount Zion (see D&C 84:2–3). It was to be a city of holiness, one that included a house of the Lord (see D&C 57:1–5).

The plat, or plan, for this city was likewise revealed to the Prophet. Wilford Woodruff recorded that the plat for the city of Kirtland, Ohio—which paralleled the one for the New Jerusalem—"was given [to Joseph Smith] by vision."[2] On 25 June 1833 Joseph had this plan rendered on paper, and after having explanatory notes

THE PROPHET HAD LITTLE OPPORTUNITY FOR EDUCATION DURING HIS YOUTH, but as an adult he tried to compensate for his deficiency. By February 1844 he had studied German, Latin, French, Hebrew, Chaldean, Dutch, and Greek. As a university regent, Joseph Smith was one of the persons responsible for "all matters appertaining to education, from common schools up to the highest branches of a most liberal collegiate course." The aim of the regents was "to teach . . . children wisdom" and "to instruct them in all . . . knowledge and learning, in the arts, sciences, and learned professions." They believed that education enhanced individual happiness and provided for the public good (*HC*, 4:269).

Joseph Smith:

The City Charter of Nauvoo is of my own plan and device. I concocted it for the salvation of the Church, and on principles so broad that every honest man might dwell secure under its protective influence without distinction of sect or party.

HC, 4:249.

THE PLAT OF THE CITY OF ZION IN JACKSON COUNTY, Missouri. Joseph Smith was commanded in a vision to establish this holy city at a specific location (see *HC,* 2:254), and he was also shown by vision how such a municipality should be laid out (see Wilford Woodruff, journal, 6 April 1837, LDS Church Archives, Salt Lake City, UT). The Prophet anticipated that this pattern would be employed repeatedly until all the earth became a Zion society (see *HC,* 1:358–59).

written in the margins, he sent it off to the presiding brethren in Jackson County, Missouri, as a guide for their building endeavors.

The plan called for a city one square mile in size with an anticipated population of between 15,000 and 20,000 people. It was to be mostly composed of ten-acre blocks aligned perfectly to the four cardinal directions. Each block was to be subdivided into twenty lots, each lot measuring one and a half acres. The homes in the city were to be arranged so that every other block of houses faced in a different direction, thus ensuring the privacy of the citizenry.

The city was also to have several distinct zones. Outside the city proper were to be the farmland, barns, and stables. The majority of the city itself was designated as residential living space (one brick or stone house per lot with a grove and a garden), and in the center of the city was to be a large and impressive temple complex and other municipal buildings. It was contemplated that the New Jerusalem would have not just one temple but twenty-four in all: twelve dedicated for Aaronic Priesthood purposes and twelve for the Melchizedek Priesthood.[3]

Joseph Smith envisioned that this divinely revealed city plan would eventually be utilized on the grand scale. He said, "When this square is thus laid off and supplied, lay off another in the same way, and so fill up the world in these last days."[4] As it turned out, this general plan was implemented in such places as Far West, Missouri; Nauvoo, Illinois; and Salt Lake City, Utah.

EDUCATOR

Through His authorized mouthpiece, the Lord taught the Latter-day Saints several principles regarding the importance of education. He informed them that "the glory of God is intelligence, or, in other words, light and truth" (D&C 93:36) and commanded them to "seek learning . . . by study" (D&C 88:118). He even provided a general curriculum when He instructed them to "obtain a knowledge of history, and of countries, and of kingdoms, [and] of laws of God and man" (D&C 93:53); "become acquainted with all good books, and with languages, tongues, and people" (90:15); and learn of things "in heaven and in the earth, and under the earth" (88:79). The Lord also gave the reason why He desired the Saints to acquire knowledge in the secular realm, stating that doing so would help prepare them to interact with those they contacted on their missions (see D&C 88:80).

The Prophet took these instructions on education seriously. Evidence of this can be seen in a letter that he wrote to his wife in the year 1839. He admonished her with regard to their children by saying, "Do teach them all you can, that they may have good minds, . . . teaching them right things to form their young and tender minds, that they begin in right paths."[5] Joseph also carried out the Lord's commands on a much larger scale when he organized and authorized several Schools of the Prophets and Schools of the Elders both in Kirtland, Ohio, and in Jackson County, Missouri. Classes taught in these adult schools included English grammar, theology, government, Hebrew, math, philosophy, geography, history, and literature. President Smith not only presided at the Kirtland schools but also served as one of the teachers.[6]

When the headquarters of the Church of Jesus Christ was being relocated to Nauvoo, Illinois, Joseph Smith was involved in petitioning the state government for permission to set up a "seminary of learning" within the city limits.[7] Permission was eventually granted, the University of the City of Nauvoo was organized, and Joseph Smith was chosen as one of twenty-three men who sat on its board of regents. The Prophet did more than help administer the school; he was a student as well. He attended music classes taught at the university by Professor Gustavus Hills.[8]

STOREKEEPER

Joseph Smith's family had a history of storekeeping. Even before Joseph was born, his father had been one of the partners in a mercantile venture in the town of Randolph, Vermont. Though it was a small operation, this store engaged in some limited overseas exporting.[9] One person who knew several members of the Smith family when they resided in Palmyra, New York, indicated that they ran a "shop" of some kind in the area. In this business the Smiths reportedly sold things such as "gingerbread, pies, boiled eggs, root beer, and other like notions of traffic."[10]

On 5 January 1842 Joseph Smith Jr. opened an establishment of his own that became known as the Red Brick Store. It was located just a little south and west of his home in Nauvoo and was one of about thirty-five stores that could be found scattered throughout the frontier river city. Brother Joseph's building was "somewhat spacious . . . for a country store" and had a ten-foot-high ceiling. The main area was "devoted exclusively to shelves and drawers," but the "counters, drawers, and pillars present[ed] a very respectable representation of oak, mahogany and marble," especially for a "backwoods establishment."[11] The walls of the store had been painted a rich red color by a convert from England,[12] and everywhere one looked one could find goods transported from New Orleans and St. Louis—thirteen wagonloads worth.[13] Joseph judged his assortment of consumer items to be "tolerably good."[14]

The daybook of the Red Brick Store, which is still in existence, reports the transactions that took place, as well as the prices at which supplies were being sold in the early 1840s. They include the following:

One yard of ribbon	13¢
One pound of sugar	10¢
Three dozen eggs	19¢
One cradle scythe	$1.50
One shovel	$1.25
One whip	$1.50
One pair of shoes	$2.25
One pair of boots	$4.50 [15]

Joseph reported that when his Nauvoo establishment was first opened it was "filled to overflowing," and he "stood behind the counter all day, dealing out goods as steady as any clerk you ever saw." He indicated in a letter to Edward Hunter that he enjoyed this kind of labor because he loved to "wait upon the Saints, and be a servant to all."[16]

By 20 December 1843, however, the Prophet had turned the management of the Red Brick Store over to two gentlemen by the names of Butler and Lewis. It appears that there were three reasons for taking this course of action. First, Joseph had other responsibilities in the community that called for a considerable amount of his time and energy. Second, the store system in the nineteenth century allowed several different types of payment—including cash, credit, and trade—and as a naturally kindhearted man, the Prophet was willing to extend credit to many people who desired to obtain goods from him. Unfortunately, some of Joseph's customers apparently thought that because he was a man of God, he ought to be willing to forgive his debtors— so they never bothered to pay back what they owed him. The resulting financial strain probably forced Joseph to reconsider the overall profitability of his business and the advisability of continuing on in the same course. Third, some people simply could not separate the man from the prophet. If Joseph would not do business with them in a manner that was to their advantage, they decided he could not possibly be a true prophet of God, and they therefore apostatized from the Church. Such a thing was absolutely intolerable, for in Joseph's mind the people were more valuable than the goods.[17]

Brigham Young explained the causes of some of Joseph Smith's business problems in this manner:

Joseph . . . buys twenty thousand dollars worth of goods . . . and commences to trade. In comes one of the brethren, "Brother Joseph, let me have a frock pattern for my wife." What if Joseph says, "No, I cannot without the money"? The consequence would be, "He is no prophet," says James.

Pretty soon Thomas walks in. "Brother Joseph, will you trust me for a pair of boots?"

"No, I cannot let them go without the money."

"Well," says Thomas, "Brother Joseph is no prophet; I have found *that* out, and I am glad of it."

After a while, in comes Bill and Sister Susan. Says Bill, "Brother Joseph, I want a shawl, I have not got the money, but I wish you to trust me a week or a fortnight."

Well, brother Joseph thinks the others have gone and apostatized, and he don't know but these goods will make the whole Church do the same, so he lets Bill have a shawl. Bill walks off with it and meets a brother. "Well," says he, "what do you think of brother Joseph?"

"Oh, he is a first-rate man, and I fully believe he is a prophet. See here, he has trusted me this shawl."

Richard says, "I think I will go down and see if he won't trust me some."

In walks Richard. "Brother Joseph, I want to trade about twenty dollars."

"Well," says Joseph, "these goods will make the people apostatize; so over they go, they are of less value than the people."

Richard gets his goods.

Another comes in the same way to so make a trade of twenty-five dollars, and so it goes. Joseph was a first-rate fellow with them all the time, provided he never would ask them to pay him. In this way it is easy for us to trade away a first-rate store of goods, and be in debt for them.

JD, 1:215; italics in original.

JOSEPH SMITH ENJOYED RUNNING HIS OWN MERCANTILE BUSINESS AND WAS PLEASED NOT ONLY TO SERVE the residents of Nauvoo in a civic capacity but also to offer them the bounties of civilization out on the edge of the American frontier. Jane Manning James recalled how the Prophet insisted that his wife take her down to the Red Brick Store and replace articles of clothing that had been stolen from her during an arduous trek to Nauvoo.

NEWSPAPER EDITOR

In August 1837 Sidney Rigdon announced on the pages of the *Messenger and Advocate* that it would soon cease to be produced and its replacement would be a new monthly periodical called the *Elders' Journal,* with Joseph Smith Jr. serving as editor. One of the reasons for the changeover in papers was the fact that Warren Parrish, the editor of the *Messenger and Advocate,* had become critical of the Church's leadership—in print—and had also decided to quit running the paper.

A REPLICA OF THE PRESS used to print the local newspaper in Nauvoo, Illinois. The press and type that were being used by the LDS Church in Far West, Missouri, had to be buried when a mob threatened the city in 1838. These items were later dug up and transported to Nauvoo, where they were used in the production of the *Times and Seasons* (see *HC,* 4:398).

THE *TIMES AND SEASONS* printing office was located on the corner of Water and Bain Streets, not far from the Prophet's Nauvoo home. The book of Abraham and other important documents were published on the pages of this Church newspaper while President Smith was serving as its editor. A subscription to the paper was two dollars per year—in advance.

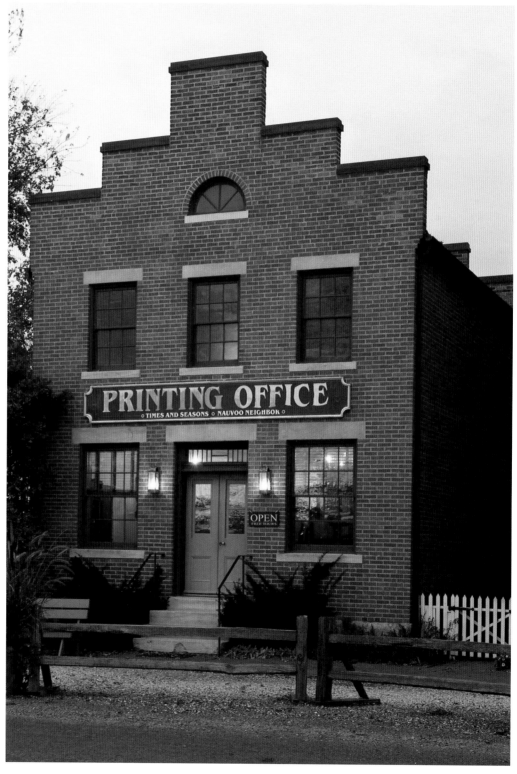

The *Elders' Journal* first came off the press in Kirtland, Ohio, in October 1837, with Thomas B. Marsh as publisher. It was designed to be "a vehicle of communication for all the elders of the Church" so that they could make known "all things pertaining to their mission." A short remark by editor Smith shows the philosophical foundation upon which the paper rested. It reads, "We calculate to pursue a different course from that of our predecessor in the editorial department. We will endeavor not to scandalize our own citizens, especially when there is no foundation in truth for doing so." The Prophet continued to act in his editorial station until August 1838, when the paper went out of print in Far West, Missouri, due to mob persecution and violence.[18]

The main newspaper in Nauvoo, Illinois, was called the *Times and Seasons.* It had originally been established and edited by Ebenezer Robinson and Don Carlos Smith (the Prophet's youngest brother) in the basement of a warehouse. It began circulation in November 1839, and its stated purpose was to report "all general information respecting the Church."[19] After Don Carlos died in 1841, Church authorities became dissatisfied with the way the paper was being run. The 15 February 1842 edition of the newspaper was the first to list Joseph Smith as the new managing editor, and in it he expressed the hope that the God of Israel would guide his heart and direct his pen as he took over the editorial chair.[20] In the 1 March issue, Joseph printed a notice wherein he acknowledged responsibility for the paper's content.[21] The Prophet was aided in his newspaper duties by Elder John Taylor, who acted in the capacity of assistant editor, and Elder Wilford Woodruff, who served as the business manager.

Several important documents were published on the pages of the *Times and Seasons* while the Prophet had charge of it. In the 1 March 1842 edition of the paper, the Church President published a letter written to John Wentworth that included thirteen short statements about the religion of the Latter-day Saints. This doctrinal sketch is now known as the Articles of Faith. This issue of the paper also carried the first of the scriptural material known as the book of Abraham. The present contents of the book of Abraham were published by the 16 March issue. (One year later John Taylor said that the Prophet had promised to provide further extracts from the book.[22]) During this period of his editorial career, Joseph also wrote and published instructions related to the building of the Nauvoo Temple, a doctrinal discourse on baptism for the dead, and a lengthy article on avoiding deception by unholy spirits.

Joseph's editorship of the *Times and Seasons* was a relatively short-lived affair. He served in this capacity for only about nine months. When the 15 November 1842 issue was put to the press, John Taylor was listed as the new managing editor.

LIEUTENANT GENERAL

When the Latter-day Saints took refuge in the state of Illinois in the late 1830s, they were required by law to bear arms and serve in a militia that was subject to both the governor of the state and the U.S. president. However, because the mobs of Missouri had plundered the Saints of most of their firearms, they petitioned the government of Illinois for a stock of weapons in order to fulfill the legal requirement.

Even though Joseph Smith was legally exempt from military duty due to his lame left leg (caused by a boyhood operation to remove some of the bone), he told the Saints that he would set an example for them by becoming part of a company of soldiers. Their response was that they were also willing to do their civic duty, but they desired to be formed into an independent company because persecution from Missouri militias had made them distrustful of state-sponsored armed forces. They also wanted President Smith to be their leader.[23] The Illinois legislature agreed to the formation of an independent city militia when they granted the powers sought after in the Nauvoo City Charter. Hence, a unique military unit was born. On 4 February 1841 Joseph Smith was elected as the lieutenant general of this body, which was named the Nauvoo Legion. His certificate of commission, signed by Illinois governor Thomas Carlin, reads:

> Know ye that Joseph Smith, having been duly
> elected to the office of lieutenant general,
> Nauvoo Legion, of the militia of the State of
> Illinois, I, Thomas Carlin, governor of said

SUTCLIFFE MAUDSLEY'S PAINTING OF LIEUTENANT General Joseph Smith in his Nauvoo Legion uniform (ca. 1842). This image may have been created by using a mechanical device called a pantograph. A comparison of this artwork with an 1844 mask made of the Prophet's face shows it to be a very accurate likeness.

LIEUTENANT GENERAL JOSEPH SMITH'S NAUVOO Legion sash, scabbard, and eagle-headed sword. A comparison of this sword with the one pictured in the Sutcliffe Maudsley painting leads to the conclusion that they are likely one and the same object (note the painted patterns on the blade, the design of the crosspiece, and the scallop shell that sits directly below it).

state, do commission him lieutenant-general of the Nauvoo Legion, to take rank from the fifth day of February, 1841. He is, therefore, carefully and diligently to discharge the duties of said office, by doing and performing all manner of things thereunto belonging; and I do strictly require all officers and soldiers under his command to be obedient to his orders: and he is to obey such orders and directions as he shall receive, from time to time, from the commander-in-chief or his superior officer.[24]

The Prophet provided some interesting insights into the makeup and aims of the Nauvoo Legion. He said that it was "not . . . exclusively a 'Mormon' military association, but a body of citizen soldiers, organized (without regard to political preferences or religious sentiments) for the public defense, the general good, and the preservation of law and order." The legion's intended job was "to save . . . innocent, unoffending citizens from the iron grasp of the oppressor and perpetuate and sustain . . . free institutions against

misrule, anarchy, and mob violence." No other views, said the Prophet, were to be "entertained or tolerated."[25]

Lieutenant General Smith was proud to serve in this military unit. On 4 July 1841 the legion participated in an Independence Day celebration, and after reviewing their formations he gave "an eloquent and patriotic speech to the troops, and strongly testified of his regard for [the] national welfare, and his willingness to lay down his life in defense of his country."[26] He was equally proud of the men for whom he had charge. In 1843 he remarked on their improvement in tactical knowledge and discipline and called them "the pride of Illinois, one of its strongest defenses, and a great bulwark of the western country."[27]

Large numbers of men served under Joseph Smith's military command. By the mid-1840s the Nauvoo Legion consisted of roughly five thousand men, making it second in size only to the United States Army.[28] The citizens of the surrounding counties enjoyed watching the legion when it was practicing or on parade. On 4 July 1842 the weather in Nauvoo was not very agreeable. Nevertheless, that did not prevent "an immense number of spectators" from being present to witness the legion's revolutions, "including the passengers of three steamers from the neighboring cities and villages."[29] Said Sarah Burbank, "I have seen Joseph in his regiment unit on his black horse," training his soldiers, with "sword in hand as they marched with drum and fifes." Sitting on the ground with many others who were watching him, she thought that he looked grand in his uniform and feathered hat.[30] Mary Clark was equally enchanted by such a scene. She specifically remembered Joseph's "prancing black horse that seemed to keep time with the music of the band."[31]

PRESIDENTIAL CANDIDATE

The Latter-day Saints were ruthlessly driven from their Missouri homes in 1838 under a state-sponsored "Extermination Order." In 1839 and 1840 Joseph Smith personally appealed for redress to Congress and to the president of the United States. But his pleas went unheeded. The Prophet reported President Martin Van Buren's reply as being something like the following: "Your cause is just, but I can do nothing for you."[32]

When the next presidential election approached, the Prophet wrote to all of the candidates in an attempt to discern their stance in regard to the Latter-day Saints. He also wanted to know whether each aspirant, if elected, would support the constitutional rights of the members of the Church of Jesus Christ. None of the respondents

JOSEPH SMITH'S OFFICE in the Nauvoo Mansion House was the scene of many important meetings. The Prophet gathered in this room with other Church leaders in order to discuss his candidacy for president of the United States. It was believed that if the Prophet were able to ascend to this high station the Saints would finally be protected from mobocracy and receive redress for the losses that they had suffered.

pledged their support. Henry Clay, who was ultimately chosen as President Van Buren's electoral challenger, told the Saints that if they wanted redress for the wrongs done to them, they had better "go to Oregon" and "get justice from the Indians!"[33]

On 29 January 1844 Joseph Smith met in his Nauvoo Mansion House office with the Quorum of the Twelve Apostles and a few other men. It was decided in this meeting that they could not in good conscience vote for either presidential nominee. Willard Richards then moved that Joseph Smith Jr. run as a presidential candidate on an independent electoral ticket. The idea was unanimously sanctioned by those present, and Joseph responded by saying, "[W]e have had Whig and Democratic presidents long enough: we want a president of the United States. If I ever get into the presidential chair, I will protect the people in their rights and liberties."[34]

By 7 February 1844 the Prophet had written a twelve-page pamphlet on his political views. It was called "General Smith's Views of the Powers and Policy of the Government of the United States." In it he stated that if elected to the presidential office, he would honor the paths taken by such venerated fathers of freedom as Franklin, Washington, Adams, Jefferson, Madison, Monroe, and Jackson. He further said that he advocated such things as the abolition of slavery, removal of archaic laws, prison reform, creation of a national banking system, reduction of government offices (in pay, number, and power), and universal peace. The united voice of the people, in Joseph's opinion, was the only sovereign or king that should rule.[35]

The Prophet sent representatives throughout the United States with his pamphlet and instructed them to electioneer on his behalf. And he reminded the Saints why he was doing all of this. He said,

> I would not have suffered my name to have been used by my friends on anywise as president of the United States, or candidate for that office, if I and my friends could have had the privilege of enjoying our religious and civil rights as American citizens, even those rights which the Constitution guarantees unto all her citizens alike. But this as a people we have been denied from the beginning. Persecution has rolled upon our heads from time to time, from portions of

> the United States, like peals of thunder, because of our religion; and no portion of the government as yet has stepped forward for our relief. And in view of these things, I feel it to be my right and privilege to obtain what influence and power I can, lawfully, in the United States, for the protection of injured innocence.[36]

The Prophet's formal nomination for president came at a state convention held in Nauvoo on 17 May 1844. Sidney Rigdon was announced as his running mate, and a national convention was planned for 13 July in Baltimore, Maryland. It appears that General Smith's popularity with the people in the surrounding countryside was considerable. A straw poll taken aboard a steamboat called the *Osprey* showed that he was leading both Van Buren and Clay.[37]

Despite the momentum that was building in his favor, Joseph Smith's bid for the presidency lasted for only five months. It abruptly ended on 27 June 1844, when he and his brother Hyrum were murdered by a mob of miscreants in Carthage, Illinois.

A POLL TAKEN ABOARD a Mississippi River steamboat called the *Osprey* in 1844 showed that a considerable number of people thought favorably of Joseph Smith's bid for the U.S. presidency.

CHAPTER 8

Evidences of a DIVINE CALLING

JOSEPH SMITH'S CLAIMS TO A DIVINE CALLING ARE EXTRAORDINARY IN THEIR NATURE—SO EXTRAORDINARY, IN FACT, THAT SOME PEOPLE HAVE DIFFICULTY ACCEPTING THEIR VALIDITY. Joseph understood this dilemma and said on one occasion, "I don't blame anyone for not believing my history. If I had not experienced what I have, I would not have believed it myself."[1] Yet he steadfastly maintained that he had "actually . . . been called of God" and could not back out of the work that he was engaged in, because he had absolutely no doubt of the truth.[2] According to Bishop Dennison L. Harris, the Prophet testified concerning the divine origin of his work with these words, "I am no false prophet; I am no impostor. I have had no dark revelations, I have had no revelations from the devil. I have made no revelations; I have not got anything up myself."[3]

A vast body of evidence confirms Joseph Smith's claims of receiving a divine calling. The evidence includes the testimonies of others who shared his religious experiences, spiritual gifts manifest in the Prophet, prophecies he made that were fulfilled, and divine protection provided in his behalf.

JOSEPH SMITH SAID THAT THE PRESENCE OF SPIRITUAL GIFTS AMONG THE Latter-day Saints would serve as an authenticating sign of his divinely appointed ministry. The Kirtland Temple was the site of a veritable pentecostal outpouring in the spring of 1836. Historical records report that the types of manifestations witnessed in the temple at this time included speaking in tongues, the sound of heavenly choirs, the appearance of angels, and visions.

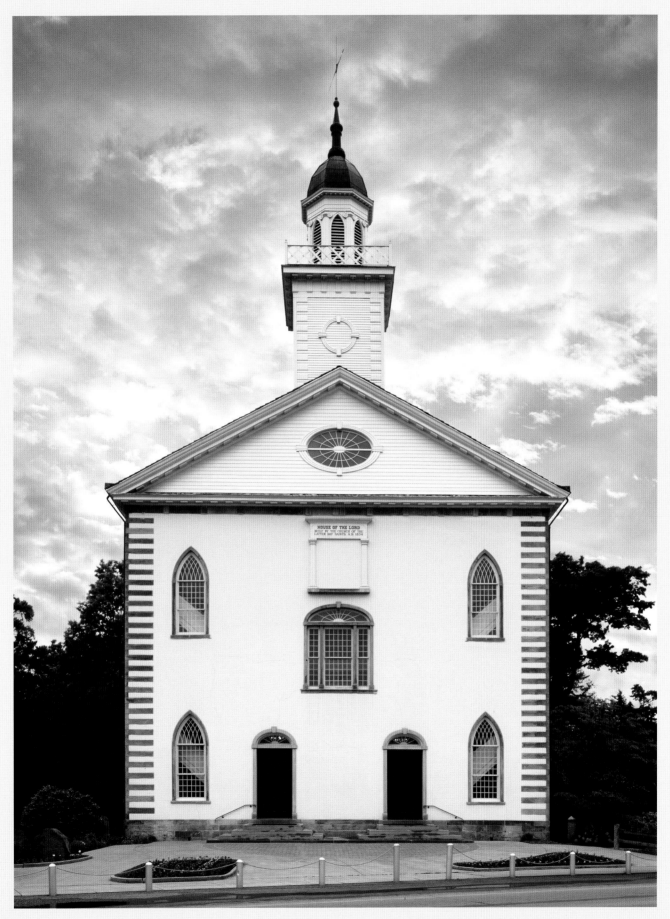

MELCHIZEDEK PRIESTHOOD PULPITS inside the Kirtland Temple, where the events of D&C 110 took place. Notice that the yoke-shaped sacrament table on the bottom level was cut in two so that when the room was divided down the center by a large veil the Lord's Supper could still be administered to the people in each compartment.

THE LORD JESUS CHRIST appeared in the Kirtland Temple to accept its dedication on 3 April 1836, as depicted in this painting by Walter Rane. Oliver Cowdery was a witness to this appearance and also to the subsequent visitations of other heavenly beings who restored keys of power and authority related to the fullness of temple ordinances (see D&C 110).

OTHER WITNESSES

The biblical pattern for establishing the truth is known as the law of witnesses. This law is expressed in 2 Corinthians 13:1, which reads, "In the mouth of two or three witnesses shall every word be established" (see also Deut. 19:15). The law of witnesses can be applied to the claims made by the Prophet Joseph Smith. There are many witnesses that could be called forward to establish the reality of the Prophet's claims, for he notes in the *History of the Church* that there were times when people around him shared in the ministering of angels and the viewing of visions.[4] A few of these types of shared experiences are cited here.

SHARED VISITATIONS

Joseph Smith boldly claimed that he was visited by various heavenly beings, including Deity, Old and New Testament religious figures, and prophets who are mentioned in Book of Mormon texts.[5] There are several cases where other people were present during these visitations, and they thus stand as sure witnesses to the reality of the Prophet's experiences.

Oliver Cowdery, who served as the scribe for the majority of the Book of Mormon translation, was present when both the Aaronic and Melchizedek Priesthoods were restored to the earth in 1829. His testimony regarding these occurrences is clear and concise. He stated on 21 October 1848, "I was present with Joseph when

THE ANTHON Transcript, shown here, displays hieroglyphics copied from the golden plates of the Book of Mormon. Some sources claim that this is the same document that Martin Harris took to show scholars in eastern cities in 1828. It is believed that the word "Caractors" is in the handwriting of Joseph Smith.

an holy angel from God came down from heaven and conferred or restored the Aaronic Priesthood and said at the same time that it should remain upon the earth while the earth stands. I was also present with Joseph when the Melchizedek Priesthood was conferred by the holy angels of God."[6] On another occasion Oliver confirmed that John the Baptist had conferred the Aaronic Priesthood on him and Joseph and that the Apostle Peter was the person who gave them the Melchizedek Priesthood. He also mentioned that he and Joseph were allowed to "look down through time, and witness the effects these two [priesthoods] must produce."[7]

Oliver Cowdery was also present in the Kirtland Temple when the keys pertaining to the fullness of temple work in the last dispensation were returned to the earth on 3 April 1836. During this sacred event, Joseph and Oliver saw the Lord Jesus Christ standing on the breastwork of the western pulpits as He accepted the dedication of the temple. They also saw Moses, Elias, and Elijah, who restored specific keys (see D&C 110).

Another visitation others shared with Joseph Smith was the appearance of an angel in Fayette, New York, to the Three Witnesses of the Book of Mormon. This was actually two visitations, because Martin Harris saw the angel separately from David Whitmer and Oliver Cowdery. In addition to their published testimony in the Book of Mormon, there were many other times when these three men bore witness to their experience. Edward Stevenson, for instance, "often heard [Oliver Cowdery] bear a faithful testimony to the restoration of the gospel by the visitation of an angel, in whose presence he stood in company with the Prophet Joseph Smith and David Whitmer. He testified that he beheld the plates, the leaves being turned over by the angel, whose voice he heard."[8] Thomas B. Marsh interviewed David Whitmer and "enquired seriously of [him] if it was true that he had seen the angel, according to his testimony as one of the witnesses of the Book of Mormon. He replied as sure as there is a God in heaven, he saw the angel according to his testimony in that book."[9] William Pilkington said of Martin Harris, "He told me many, many times that he did stand in the presence of the angel of the Lord, with Joseph Smith, and heard the voice of God from heaven declare that everything the angel told them was true and that the Book of Mormon was translated correctly."[10]

SHARED VISIONS

There were several people who were privileged to see visions at the same time that Joseph Smith did. One of the better-known instances was the vision of the three degrees of glory, now published as section 76 of the Doctrine and Covenants. Sidney Rigdon saw everything that Joseph Smith saw during this extended manifestation, but twelve other people were also present in the room. Philo Dibble, who "saw the glory and felt the power, but did not see the vision," reported what took place.

Joseph would, at intervals, say: "What do I see?" as one might say while looking out of the window and beholding what all in the room could not see. Then he would relate what he had seen or what he was looking at. Then Sidney replied, "I see the same." Presently Sidney would say, "What do I see?" and would repeat what he had seen or was seeing, and Joseph would reply, "I see the same."

This manner of conversation was repeated at short intervals to the end of the vision, and during the whole time not a word was spoken by any other person. Not a sound nor motion made by anyone but Joseph and Sidney, and it seemed to me that they never moved a joint or limb during the time I was there, which I think was over an hour, and to the end of the vision.

Joseph sat firmly and calmly all the time in the midst of a magnificent glory, but Sidney sat limp and pale, apparently as limber as a rag, observing which, Joseph remarked, smilingly, "Sidney is not used to it as I am."[11]

Lorenzo D. Wasson asked David Hale (brother of the Prophet's wife),

Where is the man that knows that he is propagating a religion that is false, and founded on hypocrisy, that will not forsake it when placed at the point of fifty bayonets and summoned to renounce his faith or die imprisoned for months, . . . and tarred and feathered and various other fiendish, devilish tortures inflicted upon him? I ask where is the man that will stand . . . if he is not sure he is doing the works of righteousness? There is not a man in Christendom among all the sons and daughters of Adam, I will venture to say.

Lorenzo Wasson to David Hale, February 1841, LDS Church Archives, Salt Lake City, UT.

In section 95 of the Doctrine and Covenants, the Lord said that He would show the pattern for building the Kirtland Temple to three individuals who were to be appointed and ordained unto that power (see v. 14). The three men appointed to this privilege were the First Presidency of the Church: Joseph Smith Jr., Sidney Rigdon, and Frederick G. Williams. President Williams, who was interviewed about this manifestation while standing inside the finished structure, related the following.

> Joseph received the word of the Lord for him to take his two counselors Williams and Rigdon and come before the Lord, and He would show them the plan or model of the house to be built. We went upon our knees, called on the Lord, and the building appeared within viewing distance: I being the first to discover it. Then all of us viewed it together. After we had taken a good look at the exterior, the building seemed to come right over us, and the makeup of this hall seems to coincide with what I there saw to a minutia.[12]

There are several accounts of people who saw heavenly beings along with Joseph Smith but did not have any interaction with them. One such case occurred inside the Kirtland Temple during a meeting at which the Prophet was speaking. Elam Cheney noticed that during his discourse the Prophet kept looking up, as if he were peering at somebody. Elam looked around and saw three men standing at each side of the room. They were wearing white clothing, white caps, and white moccasins. Elam brought these men to the attention of his mother, but she was unable to see them.[13]

Zebedee Coltrin reported two incidents of the same nature. In one, he was with Joseph Smith and Oliver Cowdery when all three witnessed the opening of the heavens and saw Adam and Eve seated upon a golden throne.[14] In the other, Zebedee was present during a meeting of the School of the Prophets in Kirtland, Ohio. Joseph had given the group some instructions on prayer, and while they were praying individually, a personage was seen passing through the room. Joseph asked if the others had seen Him and then stated that it was the Savior, the Son of God.

Joseph told the brethren to continue their prayers, and soon another personage appeared. But this Being was different. He was surrounded by a brilliant light or fire, and the power that accompanied His presence could be felt in the marrow of the bone. Joseph announced that this was God the Father. Brother Coltrin testified, "I saw Him."[15]

THE SCHOOL OF THE PROPHETS ROOM WAS LOCATED on the second story of the Newel K. Whitney Store (shown to right) in Kirtland, Ohio. In this room Joseph Smith and several other men simultaneously saw the Father and the Son. Zebedee Coltrin recalled that when the Father appeared he felt as though the marrow in his bones would melt.

SPIRITUAL GIFTS

Another sign of Joseph Smith's divine calling is the fact that the gifts of the Spirit described in the Bible were manifest in him and the Saints. The gifts of the Spirit were restored to the earth through his instrumentality. The bestowal of the authentic gift of the Holy Ghost enabled the Saints to enjoy these choice blessings once more. "If you will obey the gospel with honest hearts," said Joseph, "I promise you in the name of the Lord, that the gifts promised by our Savior will follow you. And by this you may prove me to be a true servant of God."[16] The historical records of the Church abound in examples of Latter-day Saints being blessed with spiritual gifts,[17] but a few instances from the life of Joseph Smith will suffice to establish the point that he exercised the powers of heaven.

Joseph Smith is known to have spoken in tongues on several occasions.[18] After hearing Brigham Young exercise this gift in November 1832, Joseph said, "Brethren, this tongue that we have heard is the gift of God, for He has made it known unto me, and I shall never oppose anything that comes from Him. I feel the spirit that Brother Brigham has manifested in this gift of tongues, and I wish to speak myself in the tongue that it will please the Lord to give me." He then proceeded to speak in an unknown language and explained, "Brethren, this is the language of our father Adam while he dwelt in Eden; and the time will again come, that when the Lord brings again Zion, the Zion of Enoch, this people will then all speak the language which I have just spoken."[19]

The episode of the Prophet healing many individuals in Nauvoo by the laying on of hands is fairly well known,[20] but one of those healings is particularly significant because it strongly suggests that an actual heavenly power was being used and the person didn't recover simply because of the Prophet's personal charisma. Benjamin Brown wrote,

> My family, with myself, were also taken sick, and I laid so for two or three weeks. I was so far gone that I was quite senseless, and all thought I was dying. Doubtless I should have died, but one day Joseph Smith was passing by my door, for I had managed to procure a house, and was called in, and, as I was afterwards informed, laid his hands upon me, and commanded me to rise and walk in the name of the Lord. The first thing I knew was that I found myself walking on the floor, perfectly well, and within ten minutes afterwards I was out of the house visiting my daughter, whom I had not seen for nearly a month. I felt so full of joy and happiness, that I was greatly surprised that everyone else was not as full of praise as myself. This was the second time that I had been healed instantly by the power of God, through His servants.

[Asa Lyman] was one of the stonemasons who built the Kirtland Temple. He had been afflicted with epileptic fits for two years. The Prophet Joseph told him if he went to work on that temple he should not be afflicted with a fit. He accordingly went to work, when it was six feet high, and continued until the top stone, fifty feet high, was put on, and all the time did not have one fit.

George A. Smith, report
on 11 September 1847 death of Asa Lyman,
Mormon Biography File, LDS Church Archives,
Salt Lake City, UT.

This man, Joseph Smith, was the one that the world says was an impostor, and a false prophet, and either deny that he ever performed any miracle, or, if any are too well attested to be denied, attribute them to the power of the imagination over the body. Was it the power of imagination over the body, that cured me, when I did not even hear Joseph's voice, or know that any operation on my behalf was going on, until I found myself well? The honest in heart will judge righteously.[21]

There are other stories of Joseph healing people by the power of God that bear recital. David Whitmer once accompanied the Prophet to visit a woman who had lost her mental faculties to the point where she could no longer recognize her own friends. But after the two men laid their hands on her and commanded her in the name of Jesus Christ to regain her senses, she was immediately restored to her right mind.[22] Jared Carter reported that the Prophet instantly healed Carter's youngest child simply by saying, in the name of the Lord, that the child would be healed because of Brother Carter's faith. On the same day a woman was healed of her blindness through Joseph's instrumentality.[23]

A story related by William Huntington shows that Joseph Smith even fulfilled the expectation of the Savior that His servants would have power to raise the dead (see Matt. 10:8; 4 Ne. 1:5; D&C 124:100). Like many of those who lived in Nauvoo in 1839, William became sick, but he grew continually weaker until he lost mobility in his limbs. He eventually lost his ability to speak. Finally his spirit left his body, and he could see what was going on in the room from the vantage point of the ceiling. He watched as people mourned his death below, but then Joseph Smith and two other men entered the chamber that his body occupied. These three men unitedly laid their hands on William's head, and as Joseph began to pray, William felt his spirit being drawn back into his lifeless body. By the time Joseph said amen, William could feel his physical senses again, and he sat up in the bed and asked for some food. In the conversation that followed, Joseph confirmed that the people who were present had witnessed a man being raised from the dead.[24]

FULFILLED PROPHECIES

There are a great many prophecies that were uttered by Joseph Smith during his lifetime, and their fulfillment stands as yet another witness of his divine calling. The following three prophecies are remarkable not only because of their swift fulfillment, but also because Joseph Smith could not have had any power whatsoever in making them come to pass.

Mary Westover told of a weather-related incident that happened in the city of Nauvoo, Illinois, in April 1844.

The most striking thing I remember of [Joseph Smith] was a prophecy he made, which I saw fulfilled immediately. I was at the funeral service of King Follett, which was held in the Nauvoo Grove. There was a heavy thunderstorm [that] arose and as it increased the people became frightened and started to go home; but

before anyone left the Prophet arose and told the multitude if they would remain still and pray in their hearts, the storm would not molest them in their services.

They did as they were bidden, the storm divided over the grove. I well remember how it was storming on all sides of the grove, yet it was as calm around us as if there was no sign of a storm so nearby.[25]

The Prophet Joseph Smith published the following account of a plague that struck the members of Zion's Camp in June 1834.

While we were refreshing ourselves and [our] teams about the middle of the day, I got up on a wagon wheel, called the people together, and said that I would deliver a prophecy. After giving the brethren much good advice, exhorting them to faithfulness and humility, I said the Lord had revealed to me that a scourge would come upon the camp in consequence of the fractious and unruly spirits that appeared among them, and they should die like sheep with the rot; still, if they would repent and humble themselves before the Lord, the scourge, in a great measure, might be turned away; but, as the Lord lives, the members of this camp will suffer for giving way to their unruly temper.[26]

Records indicate that the promised scourge came in the form of cholera. Sixty-eight people reportedly contracted the disease, and about a dozen died from its effects.

In the fall of 1833 Joseph Smith was preaching a sermon in Kirtland, Ohio, and prophesied that within forty days the stars would fall from heaven. A skeptic in the audience wrote the prediction down so he could prove that Joseph was a false prophet when the time had expired. After thirty-nine days had passed, a Latter-day Saint named Joseph Hancock and another man were out hunting and ran into the skeptic's house. The skeptic produced his notes and asked Brother Hancock what he thought of the Church President now that the time was almost up and the prophecy unfulfilled. Brother Hancock quietly remarked that there was still some time left and that if the Prophet had uttered such a prophecy, then it would surely come to pass. That very night, as the two hunters stayed at the skeptic's house, there was an immense meteor shower in the sky. Some reports indicate that it lasted until dawn. Brother Hancock watched the face of the skeptic very closely and said that "he turned pale as death, and spoke not a word."[27]

DIVINE PROTECTION

As a prophet of God, Joseph Smith was on a divinely appointed mission, and as a consequence he was able to say, "God will always protect me until my mission is fulfilled."[28] Two incidents bear this notion out. The first occurred at Fishing River in Clay County, Missouri. Some Saints were traveling to Jackson County in the hope of regaining property stolen by mobs. They heard that they were about to be attacked by their enemies. The Prophet went into the woods and petitioned the Lord for His protection and was given an assurance that it would be granted. Everything was quiet in the camp during the night. The next evening, five armed Missourians rode into the Saints' camp and informed them that they would "see hell before morning" and otherwise spoke like a pack of demons. As soon as they had left, however, a thunderstorm began unleashing incessant flashes of lightning, tremendous thunder, high winds, torrential rain, and dangerous hail. Very little hail fell in the camp of the Saints, but its destructive force was so great elsewhere that it destroyed crops and cut the branches off some trees. A member of the mob was killed by a bolt of lightning during this incident, some of the gang's gunstocks broke, and some of their horses fled because they were frightened by the storm. After

being pelted all night by the relentless rain and hail and having their gunpowder thoroughly soaked, some members of the mob abandoned their plan to destroy the Mormons and left the area.[29]

The second incident concerning divine protection involves an apostate named William Law. This story illustrates the concept of divine protection so well that it bears a full recital. The Prophet asked a fourteen-year-old boy named Charles to serve as a houseboy at William Law's residence. As the young man learned of the plans of the Prophet's enemies, he was to relay that information. Sarah Stoddard, the boy's mother, recorded in her diary the following entry, dated April 1844, just two months before Joseph Smith was killed:

Charles had another faith-promoting experience last night.

Early this morning, even while the darkness still hemmed out the light of the day, Mr. Law, after he had been drinking and planning with his associates through the night, got Charles out of bed to clean and oil his gun. He said he was going to shoot the Prophet, only William Law called him "old Joe Smith." Poor Charles was frightened beyond description, but Mr. Law stood over him and prodded him with his foot when Charles hesitated through fright and anxiety. Finally, when Mr. Law was satisfied with the way the gun was working, he put one bullet in [the chamber] (he boasted he could kill the Prophet with one shot). He sent Charles to bring the Prophet.

He ran as fast as he could and delivered the message, but he begged the Prophet not to go to Mr. Law's as Mr. Law was drunk and Charles was afraid he would carry through on his threat to shoot the Prophet in cold blood.

As they walked the few blocks from the Mansion House to the Law residence, the Prophet assured Charles that no harm would come to him that day. Charles was frightened, and he said that it kept racing through his mind, "I am the one that cleaned the gun that is going to be used to kill the Prophet," until he was sick with fear. The Prophet in a final attempt to calm my dear son uttered the fateful

SARAH STODDARD RECORDED IN HER JOURNAL IN
April 1844 that her son was forced to clean a gun that was to be
used to kill Joseph Smith. The intended assassin summoned the
Prophet and aimed the weapon at his chest, but when he pulled
the trigger it misfired. President Smith then had a can placed on
a fence post and invited his enemy to try firing the gun again. This
time the powder ignited, and the bullet found its mark.

ANGUS CANNON RECALLED THAT IN JUNE 1843 JOSEPH
Smith escaped from kidnappers who intended to cross state lines
and turn him over to his fiercest foes. The Prophet climbed onto
this well on the east side of his homestead so that he could address
a large crowd of Saints that had gathered there. He held onto an
upright post with one hand, and, while swinging his hat in the air
with the other, he loudly proclaimed his gratitude to the God of
Israel for delivering him out of the hands of his enemies once
again (see *Young Woman's Journal,* vol. 17, no.12, December 1906,
546–47).

words, "Mr. Law may someday kill me, Charles, but it won't be today."

As they approached their destination, Mr. Law came staggering out of the house shouting out what he intended to do.

The Prophet said kindly and unafraid, "You sent for me, Mr. Law?" to which Mr. Law replied with oaths that now he was doing the whole a favor by disposing of the Prophet with one shot.

Calmly, the Prophet unbuttoned his shirt and bared his chest [and] then said, "I'm ready now, Mr. Law." Charles said at this point he nearly fainted. Sick fear strangled him until he was speechless and paralyzed, unable to move a muscle.

Mr. Law paced a few steps, turned, aimed, and pressed the trigger. There was complete silence. Then the air rang with profanity, and Mr. Law turned on Charles, accusing him of fixing the gun so it would not go off and threatening to kill even Charles—my innocent, frightened, but faithful son.

The Prophet, to divert Mr. Law's blame of Charles, suggested that a can be placed on a fence post for Mr. Law to take a practice shot. Relieved, Charles ran for a can and laid it on its side on the post. Mr. Law paced back, took aim, and fired. His "one shot" streaked through the exact center of the can.

Even Mr. Law was quiet, as if stunned.

The Prophet buttoned up his shirt, gave Charles a meaningful look, and then said, "If you are finished with me now, Mr. Law, I have other things needing to be done. Good morning."[30]

When Joseph Smith put together the Church's official history he recorded an incident involving divine protection. He wrote,

Towards the latter end of August [1830], in company with John and David Whitmer, and my brother Hyrum Smith, I visited the Church at Colesville, New York. Well knowing the determined hostility of our enemies in that quarter, and also knowing that it was our duty to visit the Church, we had called upon our Heavenly Father, in mighty prayer, that He would grant us an opportunity of meeting with them, that He would blind the eyes of our enemies, so that they would not know us, and that we might on this occasion return unmolested. Our prayers were not in vain, for when within a little distance of Mr. Knight's place, we encountered a large company at work upon the public road, amongst whom were several of our most bitter enemies. They looked earnest at us, but not knowing us, we passed on without interruption. That evening we assembled the Church, and confirmed them, partook of the sacrament, and held a happy meeting, having much reason to rejoice in the God of our salvation, and sing hosannas to His holy name.

HC, 1:108–9.

Such experiences substantiate Joseph Smith's claim to be an authentic prophet of God with a divinely appointed mission. The fact that a number of individuals witnessed and shared in his spiritual experiences makes an especially strong case in his favor. While Joseph was granted access to many wonderful powers and blessings, at least one was meant to be only temporary. The promise of divine protection from his enemies lasted only until his earthly task was complete. After that, he would be just like any other mortal man.

CHAPTER 9

MARTYRDOM *at* CARTHAGE JAIL

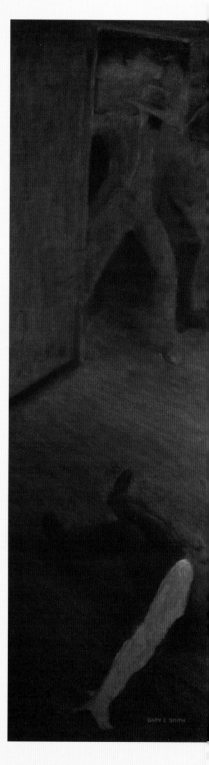

THE PROPHET JOSEPH SMITH HAD MANY ENEMIES OUTSIDE THE CHURCH, BUT HE ALSO HAD ENEMIES WITHIN. An especially troublesome dissenter was William Law, a former counselor in the First Presidency who had rejected some of the doctrines taught by the Prophet. In the early spring of 1844 Law held secret meetings in his Nauvoo residence for about two hundred people who had become disaffected with the Church. The leading participants in these gatherings intensified their vehement rhetoric against the Prophet week by week until their accusations and bitter denunciations escalated to calls for his death. It is reported that during the third meeting an oath was administered to these dissenters, wherein they agreed to give their all for the destruction of Joseph Smith and other leading authorities. Their justification was that such action was necessary "for the sake of the Church." The conspirators also threatened to kill those who were present who would not agree to take the oath.[1]

Law and his associates brought a printing press into Nauvoo on 7 May 1844 and on 7 June commenced publishing an antagonistic opposition paper that denounced Church doctrines, called for repeal of the Nauvoo City Charter, and referred to Joseph Smith as a money-hungry, immoral, heretical tyrant.[2] Nathan Cheney, writing

IN THIS PAINTING BY GARY SMITH, THE PROPHET ATTEMPTS TO REACH THE southeast window of Carthage Jail as mob members prepare to fire at him with their guns. Hyrum Smith lies dead on the floor, John Taylor (who has already been shot) seeks refuge underneath the bed, and Willard Richards attempts to fend off the attack with a cane.

a few weeks afterward, said, "They printed all the lies the devil could think of and some that he could not think of."

On 10 June, after fourteen hours of deliberation covering three separate sessions, "the city council declared [the press] to be a nuisance and ordered the city marshal to destroy it. The marshal called on eighteen or twenty men to assist him, the marshal went to

---

Eunice B. Snow:

I remember hearing the Prophet the last time he spoke in Nauvoo. He said,

"I go like a lamb to the slaughter,"

referring to the great shadow, which seemed even then to hover over his life and to foreshadow his impending doom. On the last day which he spent in Nauvoo, he passed our house with his brother Hyrum, both riding. My mother and I were standing in the dooryard, and as he passed he bowed with uplifted hat to my mother. Hyrum seemed like one in a dream, sad and despondent, taking no notice of anyone. They were on their way to the Carthage Jail, and it was the last time I saw the Prophet alive.

Woman's Exponent, vol. 39, no. 2, August 1910, 14.

---

the building and took the press and papers into the street and burned the papers, and broke the press."[3] This action, of course, enraged the dissenters—the more so because Joseph Smith was the mayor of Nauvoo. They therefore held him personally accountable for their loss.[4]

The incident with the press also angered the anti-Mormons in the surrounding countryside. Thomas Sharp, the inflammatory editor of the *Warsaw Signal,* wrote in the 12 June issue of his paper that a "war of extermination" against the Saints of Nauvoo was "inevitable." He cried out, "We have no time for comment: every man will make his own. Let it be made with POWDER and BALL!!!" Joseph's enemies brought several legal charges against him, and the governor of

Illinois, Thomas Ford, was called in to investigate the matter officially. He arrived at Carthage (the Hancock County seat) on 21 June.[5]

The next day Joseph wrote a letter to Governor Ford explaining that the legal proceedings against him and other Church officials were simply a pretext "till some bloodthirsty villain could find his opportunity to shoot" him and the others who had been charged.[6] On this same day, Hyrum Smith informed Reynolds Cahoon that a group of men was conspiring to kill the Prophet and "the Lord ha[d] warned him to flee to the Rocky Mountains to save his life."[7]

Joseph and Hyrum were convinced that murder was the ultimate aim of their enemies and that if they were put into their hands again they would surely be killed.[8] They determined that it would be best for them to cross the river and prepare provisions for a trip to the West. But a few Saints accused them of cowardice, and they were concerned that their property would end up being destroyed if the leaders left. They went to Joseph's wife and convinced her to write a letter to the Prophet requesting him to return. Joseph's response to the petition was, "If my life is of no value to my friends it is of none to myself." After consulting together, Joseph and Hyrum decided to return and face their enemies and, in Joseph's estimation, certain death.[9]

While Joseph was in Montrose, Iowa, preparing for his journey, he had a prophetic dream of things to come. He informed William W. Phelps that in this night vision he and Hyrum went aboard a steamboat that was anchored in an ocean bay. Soon afterward the boat caught fire, and they jumped overboard, trying their faith at walking on the water. At first they sank up to their knees, but as they gained more faith, they were able to walk on top of the water. The boat burning in the east drifted into the adjoining town, which also

---

THE DIMLY LIT DUNGEON OF CARTHAGE JAIL, WHICH is actually on the second floor of the building (at the top of the stairs). After jailer George W. Stigall heard stories about mob activity in the town, he suggested to his Mormon prisoners that they would be safer in this room. Joseph Smith acknowledged their intention to go into the dungeon after supper, but the sudden assault of the mob on the jail prevented them from doing so. Members of a lynch mob fired their weapons at this room when they first gained entry into the jail, supposing that Joseph Smith and other Church leaders were being held here.

caught fire and was destroyed while the inhabitants looked on in horrified fright. Joseph and Hyrum began walking toward the west and were soon out of sight of land, but the ocean was motionless beneath their feet. The rays of the sun shone brightly upon them, and they forgot all about their earthly troubles. Just then, they heard the voice of their brother Samuel coming from the east. He approached and explained that he had been lonely and had decided to go with them across the mighty deep. The three brothers continued their journey together and shortly thereafter came upon the western shore of the waters, where they saw a city of unearthly beauty. "Its order and

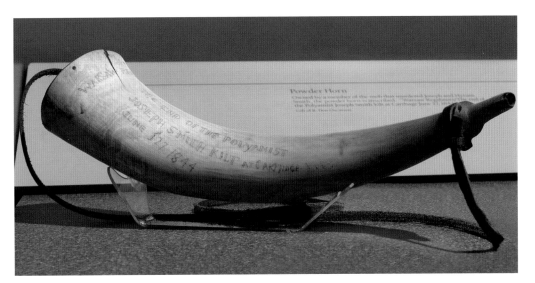

glory seemed far beyond the wisdom of man," said Joseph. A boat was launched from the shore, and as "quick as thought" it arrived and took them all on board. Once they were on the ship, they were warmly welcomed and heard "music such as is not of earth." When they arrived on the shore, they could see that the light of God was shining throughout the city. Joseph said of this experience that it soothed him with a sense of peace and joy. He greeted his friends in that place and truly felt that he was in heaven.[10]

On the morning of 24 June, Joseph bade a tearful farewell to Emma and their children at the Mansion House. The Prophet, Hyrum, and sixteen others then rode off toward Carthage, but four miles west of their destination (at the Albert G. Fellows farm) they met Captain Dunn and his cavalry. Dunn produced an order from Governor Ford stating that the citizens of Nauvoo were to surrender their "State Arms" to him. The Prophet agreed to this demand and rode back to Nauvoo to see that it was fulfilled. Joseph said good-bye to his family two more times and then left Nauvoo again at 6:00 P.M. When the group arrived at the Albert G. Fellows farm the second time, the Prophet asked his friends to return to the safety of Nauvoo, but none of them would leave.[11] He arrived in Carthage, Illinois, at 11:55 P.M. and put up at the Hamilton Hotel.

The next morning Joseph met with the governor, who "pledged the faith of the State" that the Mormons would be protected. Joseph and Hyrum and other members of the Nauvoo city council then surrendered themselves to Constable Davis Bettisworth in Carthage. In the afternoon they attended an investigation of the *Nauvoo Expositor* incident and posted bail. But in the evening, Robert F. Smith, justice of the peace and captain of the Carthage Greys militia, made out a mittimus, without holding any investigation, and committed Joseph and Hyrum to jail. Dan Jones reported that this night, in the jail, both Joseph and Hyrum said that they "were

COMPOSITE PHOTOGRAPH OF THE PEPPERBOX PISTOL THAT JOSEPH SMITH USED to defend himself after Hyrum had been murdered, and the floor of the room in Carthage Jail where the brothers were killed. Joseph wounded three of his attackers as he fired the gun blindly through a partially opened door.

(OPPOSITE) THE HOLE IN THIS DOOR PANEL MARKS THE PATH OF ONE OF THE bullets that killed Hyrum Smith. The Prophet's older brother was simultaneously struck by this bullet and one that was fired from outside the jail. He fell to the floor, exclaiming, "I'm a dead man."

about to finish their race [cf. 2 Tim. 4:6–7] and go to their joy [cf. Matt. 25:21]." Jones noted that he had never seen them "so cheerful and so heavenly minded."[12]

Joseph was visited in the Carthage jailhouse by several officers and their retinue. The Prophet asked these men if he appeared to be a man who was guilty of the charges brought against him. Did he look like an enemy of mankind, a traitor to the government, a murderer, a whoremonger? One person in the group answered that Joseph did not outwardly appear to be any of these things, but they could not discern what was in his heart. In response, the Prophet admitted that was true enough, but he could see plainly what was in *their* hearts. They wanted his blood, and nothing but his spilled blood would satisfy them. He then testified that he was not being persecuted for any crimes that he had actually committed and prophesied that, inasmuch as they thirsted for blood, they would indeed behold scenes of bloodshed.[13]

On the morning of 26 June Governor Ford and one of his friends went to the jail to interview Joseph and Hyrum. It appears that all things were explained on both sides, and the governor once more assured them that they would be protected from violence. They were also told they would be taken with the governor the next morning to Nauvoo so as to ensure their safety. But later that same day Constable Bettisworth attempted to take the Smiths from the jail for examination before Robert F. Smith on a charge of treason. The jailer knew that this maneuver was illegal and initially refused to turn over the prisoners, but the Carthage Greys militia intimidated and threatened him, and he was thereby compelled to release his charges. After Bettisworth took Joseph and Hyrum before Justice of the Peace Robert F. Smith, the defense counsel decided to stop the charade by requesting subpoenas for witnesses from Nauvoo. The examination of witnesses was then fixed for noon on 27 June, and the prisoners were sent back to the jail.[14]

During the days at Carthage, a group of anti-Mormons held a meeting at the Hamilton Hotel. Delegates from every state of the Union except for three were reportedly in attendance. These men had met to "take into consideration the best way to stop Joseph and Hyrum Smith's career." Someone proposed to the gathering that if the states of Missouri and Illinois would combine to kill the Prophet, "they would not be brought to justice for it."

The conspirators were interrupted when Stephen Markham, a friend of Joseph Smith's, suddenly came up the stairs of the hotel and into the area where they were meeting.[15]

During his last night in Carthage Jail, Joseph Smith testified of his divinely appointed mission to those who were not Latter-day Saints. The historical record states that he "bore a powerful testimony to the guards of the divine authenticity of the Book of Mormon, the restoration of the gospel, the administration of angels, and that the kingdom of God was again established upon the earth, for the sake of which he was then incarcerated in that prison, and not because he had violated any law of God or man."[16]

Early the next day, 27 June, Governor Ford consulted with the military officers present and decided that he would ride into Nauvoo with Captain Dunn's forces to address the people of the city. But he changed his mind about taking the Prophet with him. In addition, he decided that all the other military units present would be disbanded, except for the Carthage Greys, who would remain behind to guard the jail.[17] Before the governor left, he was informed by recent convert Dan Jones that one of the jail guards had told him that if he didn't want to die with the Smith brothers he had better leave Carthage before sundown. But Governor Ford brushed the comment aside, saying that Jones was "unnecessarily alarmed," that the good citizens of Carthage were simply "not that cruel."[18] But that morning Joseph told one of his lawyers that "he should not live to see another day, so fully was he impressed with the belief that he would be murdered."[19]

This ominous belief was well founded. The militiamen had been informed that once Governor Ford left Carthage for Nauvoo, they would join together with the Carthage Greys and attack the building where the Smith brothers were being held. William M. Daniels, a soldier with the Warsaw, Illinois, militia, was present when the governor's order to disband the troops was read aloud. He related that instead of disbanding, they were ordered by Thomas Sharp—editor of the *Warsaw Signal* newspaper and avowed enemy of Joseph Smith—to line up in their ranks again. Sharp encouraged the militia members to kill the men in Carthage jail, but after a vote was taken, some of the men refused to participate. Yet about eighty-five of them assented to commit the murders and made their way toward the town of Carthage. During their march, these individuals were met by a member of the Carthage Greys and were informed that the governor was gone and the Smiths had to be killed quickly, before he returned.[20]

The protection available to Joseph and his associates was meager, and the guards at the front door of the jail could not be counted on for assistance in the event of an attack. That morning Cyrus Wheelock had smuggled a pepperbox pistol, a six-shooter, into the jail and had given it to the Prophet. Joseph asked Cyrus if he shouldn't keep it for his own protection, but Cyrus felt it to be an act of providence that he was not searched upon entering the structure. Joseph accepted the weapon and gave a single-shot pistol (received earlier from John S. Fullmer) to his brother Hyrum and remarked, "We may want to help the guard defend the prison." Wheelock was then requested to obtain "several more pistols or revolvers," just in case the brethren deemed it necessary to use them. John Taylor and Willard Richards, who had remained in jail with the Prophet, were armed only with walking canes.[21]

Throughout the day the prisoners felt "unusually dull and languid, with a remarkable depression of spirits." Their disposition is further described as being "gloomy and surcharged with indefinite ominous forebodings."[22] John Taylor recalled that at about quarter past three in the afternoon, Hyrum Smith asked him to sing a hymn that had recently been introduced among the Saints at Nauvoo. Elder Taylor said, "I remember Bro. Hyrum requested me to sing 'A Poor Wayfaring Man of Grief.'"[23] The tune of the song, recalled Elder Taylor, was very much in accordance with their immediate feelings,[24] but Hyrum probably wanted to listen to the words, which tell of a prisoner who is condemned to die and of "the tide of lying tongues" that speak against him (see *Hymns*, no. 29). Before Hyrum had left his Nauvoo home for the last time, he had turned down a page in the Book of Mormon at Ether 12:36–38, a passage that refers to a faithful man whose garments would be cleansed from the blood of the Gentiles and who would inherit a place in the mansions of the Father.[25]

John Taylor recalled that "after a lapse of some time," Hyrum appealed to him to sing the song once more. Elder Taylor replied, "Brother Hyrum, I do not feel like singing." Hyrum's response was, "Oh, never mind; commence singing, and you will get the spirit of it." Elder Taylor then complied with the request of a man whom he greatly respected. Soon after the song was completed, at about a quarter after five that evening, Elder Taylor was sitting at one of the front windows of the jail when he saw a number of men with painted faces coming around the corner of the building and heading for the front door and its adjacent stairway.[26]

The initial volley of gunfire, which was discharged from somewhere down the stairs, was aimed not at the eastern room where Joseph Smith, Hyrum Smith, John Taylor, and Willard Richards were located but rather at the northern room, which

THE WATER WELL ON the southeast corner of Carthage Jail. After Joseph Smith had been shot and fell more than twelve feet from the second-story window of the jail, he reportedly tried to raise himself up by the side of the well. One eyewitness said that it was here that the Prophet spoke his last words, saying, "God's will be done."

contained the cell compartment. When these shots were fired, the four men shut the door to their room and braced themselves against it, because the latch was not in usable condition. As soon as the assailants reached the landing on the second floor of the jail, they wasted no time in firing a shot through the eastern door's locking mechanism. When this occurred, Joseph, John, and Willard sprang to one side of the room, while Hyrum stepped back, directly opposite the door. Suddenly, a bullet came blasting through the wood panel of that barrier and struck Hyrum on the left side of his nose. He was simultaneously struck by another bullet through the open window behind him and fell to the floor, crying out, "I'm a dead man." His body was also shot two other times. Joseph, with a look of deep sympathy and regard on his face, knelt over the lifeless body of his brother and exclaimed, "Oh! my poor, dear brother Hyrum!" But in an instant he arose with the pepperbox pistol in hand and moved with a quick step and determined look to the door. He opened it two or three inches, stuck the gun through the opening with his left hand, and blindly pulled the trigger six times. Only three of the barrels discharged, but each of the bullets wounded a member of the murderous mob. As Joseph fired his gun, Elder Taylor stood close by him and with a sturdy hickory cane knocked down the bayonet-tipped muskets that were belching fire and lead through the door opening. Joseph called out, "That's right, Brother Taylor, parry them off as well as you can." Elder Richards did the best that he could with the cane in his possession, but he had trouble staying clear of the firing line of the rifles.

More mobbers kept crowding onto the stairway landing and shouting vulgar, demoniacal expressions. With the situation growing worse, John Taylor leapt onto

SHORTLY AFTER THE martyrdom of Joseph and Hyrum Smith, Nauvoo resident George Cannon (father of George Q. Cannon) made masks of their faces. The objects pictured here were produced by pouring plaster into the masks (Joseph on left, Hyrum on right). These are the most accurate images of Joseph and Hyrum that are known to exist (see *Ensign*, March 1981, 65–68).

the broad sill of the eastern window, only to be shot in the leg from behind. This temporarily paralyzed him, and he fell helpless on the ledge of the opening and began to slip outside. Then a bullet fired from outside struck him in the chest with great force and thrust him back into the room. Luckily for John, the bullet hit the backside of the watch that was in his vest pocket. On finding that he was able to move again, he started to crawl underneath a bed but suffered three more shots to his body.

Joseph apparently decided that Elder Taylor had had the best idea, considering the circumstances. As a last resort, he went toward the window, but as he reached it four bullets struck—two in the back, one in the right part of his chest, and one in his right collar-bone. Willard Richards, who wrote about the incident only days after it occurred, said that "he fell outward exclaiming, 'O Lord my God!'"[27]

Thomas Dixon, who was present at the martyrdom and standing only about ten steps away from the water well on the east side of the jail, where Joseph fell, testified under oath in May 1845 that the Prophet was shot

A St. Louis newspaper called the *O. S. Democrat* printed the following in regard to the deaths of Joseph and Hyrum Smith:

From all the facts now before us, we regard these homicides as nothing else than murder in cold blood—murder against the plighted faith of the chief magistrate of Illinois—murder of a character so atrocious and so unjustifiable as to leave the blackest stain on all its perpetrators, their aiders, abettors, and defenders.

HC, 7:177–78.

inside the jail, fell out the window, then "raised himself against the well curb, drew up one leg and stretched out the other, and died immediately."[28] William Terrel, also an eyewitness to these events, adds that after Joseph crawled up against the well curb, he said "in a low but distinct voice, 'God's will be done.'"[29]

William Daniels testified under oath, less than a year after the martyrdom occurred, that a short time after the shooting stopped he saw a young man approach the body of the Prophet with a pewter flute in his hand (which seems to have been mistaken by some people for a bowie knife). Then Daniels saw something very unusual: a flash of light that passed by one side of the Prophet's body. When this happened, the young man did not advance any further. Daniels indicated that this light frightened him "very much."[30]

At 8:00 A.M. on 28 June 1844, the bodies of Joseph and Hyrum Smith were placed on separate wagons, covered over with foliage so that they would be protected from the elements, and transported across the broad prairie to Nauvoo. When the wagons were within about a mile east of the temple site, they were met by thousands of mourning citizens. The bodies of the martyrs were then driven down to the Mansion House, and the assembled Saints were informed that a viewing would be held the next morning.

Joseph's and Hyrum's bodies were cleaned and dressed for burial, and then family members, relatives, and certain friends were allowed to see them. Witnesses to this scene recalled that the lamentations heard from the two men's mother, wives, and children were not only intense but also heartrending.

At 8:00 A.M. on 29 June, the doors of the Mansion House were opened to the public. During the day it was estimated that more than ten thousand people filed through the residence to pay their last respects to the Prophet and his brother. This procession continued unabated until 5:00 P.M., when the doors were closed so that family members could say their final farewells.[31]

Since it was feared that the enemies of Joseph Smith would carry through with threats to desecrate his body, it was decided that he and his brother should be buried in a secret location. Bags of sand were placed in the pine boxes that had held the coffins, and these outer containers were then loaded into a hearse and driven out to the city graveyard.

At about midnight, the bodies of Joseph and Hyrum were taken to the Nauvoo House (just south of the Nauvoo Mansion) and buried in the basement. At Emma's request, they were later reburied near the Homestead (west of the Nauvoo House), and their graves were left unmarked.[32]

CONCLUSION

ON 29 JUNE 1844 WILLIAM W. PHELPS, A LONG-TIME ASSOCIATE OF JOSEPH SMITH, STOOD AT A MEETING GROUND TO DELIVER THE FUNERAL SERMON FOR THE MARTYRS JOSEPH AND HYRUM. Even as he praised the Prophet, their hearse passed by the congregated Saints.[1] Phelps said of the latter-day seer that even though his foes had smitten him down in desperation, their deed would not stop the onward course of "Mormonism." Instead, it would "increase its spread and rapidity an hundred fold." Even though the Prophet's body was marred by physical force, he had clothed others with the eternal priesthood, and that authority remained unharmed. These individuals, said Brother Phelps, would step into Joseph's shoes and move the cause of Zion forward with mighty power.

Brother Phelps's other remarks are a fitting tribute to the life of the Prophet. He told his audience that those who read the story of Joseph's life from his birth in Sharon, Vermont, to his death in Carthage, Illinois, would see that every line and every act shone with principles of virtue. He was a man who "knew what was right and did it, independent of consequences." "He labored like the angels," said Brother Phelps, "to save this generation" from the fire that will assuredly rain down upon the wicked at the Second Coming of the Son of Man. The revelations brought forth by his hand bear witness to the fact that he came "to point out the way of life, and call upon all men to repent and be saved." "He came to give the commandments and law of the Lord . . . and teach men to improve in love and grace, that the wise among men might gather out of spiritual Babylon." Joseph came to "increase the power to bind Satan"; "he came to war against the devil." But more importantly, "he came to . . . teach men to walk in the light of the Lord." "His words lit up a sacred flame in the heart of the Saint that showed an ocean of existence unexplored by the vain philosophy of the world." "He was the agent of Jehovah"; "he was a man of God."[2]

Just one month after delivering this eulogy before the Saints of Nauvoo, Brother Phelps published a song that today is sung worldwide in memory of the man who was "blessed to open the last dispensation" of the gospel. It affirmed that Joseph Smith was called to his station by the Lord, that he remained true and faithful throughout his life, and even though he suffered a martyr's death he has "ascended to heaven" and will someday be "crowned in the midst of the prophets of old." These were comforting thoughts for the Saints at the time as they mourned their loss, but the words of this composition also have relevance for those who live now. As the song states, the Prophet Joseph Smith still retains the keys of the dispensation of the fullness of times, and his work is not yet complete. Even now, he mingles with the Holy Ones of the celestial realm and lays plans for the kingdom of God to expand on both sides of the veil. Either in time or in the ceaseless rounds of eternity, millions upon millions will come to "know 'Brother Joseph' again" and acknowledge that he was a truly remarkable man, that he was divinely appointed to an extraordinary mission, and that he delivered an inspired message for the inhabitants of the earth.[3]

PAINTING ATTRIBUTED to Norwegian artist Danquart A. Weggeland. William W. Phelps remarked at Joseph Smith's funeral that he was a man of God; a guide sent to point out the way of life and salvation; a divinely appointed agent whose mission was to teach men to "walk in the light of the Lord."

NOTES

The historical quotations found in this volume have been standardized for modern spelling, formatting, punctuation, capitalization, and grammar; however, they have been modified carefully so as to preserve their proper content and context. Short titles are used in the notes. The Church Archives of The Church of Jesus Christ of Latter-day Saints in Salt Lake City is identified as LDS Church Archives. The L. Tom Perry Special Collections, located in the Harold B. Lee Library at Brigham Young University, Provo, Utah, is identified as L. Tom Perry Special Collections. Works frequently cited have been identified by the following abbreviations:

CHC   Brigham H. Roberts. *A Comprehensive History of The Church of Jesus Christ of Latter-day Saints.* 6 vols. Salt Lake City: Deseret News Press, 1930.

HC   Brigham H. Roberts, ed. *History of The Church of Jesus Christ of Latter-day Saints.* 4th ed. 7 vols. Salt Lake City: Deseret News Press, 1965.

JD   George D. Watt, ed. *Journal of Discourses.* 26 vols. Liverpool, England: Franklin D. Richards and Sons, 1854–86.

Lucy's Book   Lavina F. Anderson, ed. *Lucy's Book: A Critical Edition of Lucy Mack Smith's Family Memoir.* Salt Lake City: Signature Books, 2001.

PWJS   Dean C. Jessee, ed. *Personal Writings of Joseph Smith.* Rev. ed. Salt Lake City: Deseret Book; Provo, UT: Brigham Young University Press, 2002.

WJS   Andrew F. Ehat and Lyndon W. Cook, eds. *The Words of Joseph Smith: The Contemporary Accounts of the Nauvoo Discourses of the Prophet Joseph.* Orem, UT: Grandin Book, 1991.

INTRODUCTION

1. *Times and Seasons,* vol. 5, no. 14, 1 August 1844, 607.

CHAPTER 1: JOSEPH SMITH'S EARLY YEARS

1. *Lucy's Book,* 294. The farm belonged to Lucy's father.
2. *PWJS,* 10.
3. *HC,* 2:289.
4. *PWJS,* 10.
5. *Lucy's Book,* 300.
6. Orson Pratt, *An Interesting Account of Several Remarkable Visions* (Edinburgh, Scotland: Ballantyne and Hughes, 1840), 3.
7. Sally Alvord, statement, in Samuel Morgan Alvord, *A Genealogy of the Descendants of Alexander Alvord, An Early Settler of Windsor, Conn., and Northampton, Mass.* (Webster, NY: A. D. Andrews, 1908), 132.
8. Orsamus Turner, *History of the Pioneer Settlement of Phelps and Gorham's Purchase, and Morris Reserve* (Rochester, NY: William Alling, 1851), 213–14.
9. See *Lucy's Book,* 344.
10. *PWJS,* 265.
11. *Lucy's Book,* 329.
12. Joseph Smith Jr. patriarchal blessing, given by Joseph Smith Sr., 9 December 1834, Kirtland, Ohio, Patriarchal Blessing Book #1, LDS Church Archives.
13. *Deseret News,* 20 January 1894.
14. Recollection of Mrs. Palmer, in "Stories from the Notebook of Martha Cox, Grandmother of Fern Cox Anderson," LDS Church Archives.
15. *Messenger and Advocate,* vol. 1, no. 3, December 1834, 40.
16. *HC,* 1:16.
17. *Deseret News,* 20 January 1894.
18. See *Ensign,* August 1985, 17.
19. See Richard L. Anderson, *Investigating the Book of Mormon Witnesses* (Salt Lake City: Deseret Book, 1981), 143; and *CHC,* 1:31–32.
20. See *Ensign,* August 1985, 17.
21. *Deseret News,* 20 January 1894.
22. Recollection of Mrs. Palmer, LDS Church Archives.

23. *HC,* 5:498.
24. Ibid., 6:56–57.
25. *PWJS,* 10.
26. Conference in Nauvoo, Illinois, 8 October 1845, General Minutes Collection, LDS Church Archives.
27. *PWJS,* 335.
28. Joseph Smith Jr. patriarchal blessing, LDS Church Archives.
29. *Lucy's Book,* 329.
30. The information in this story has been gleaned from *Lucy's Book,* 303–10; *BYU Studies* 10.4 (summer 1970): 481. For further reading, see LeRoy S. Wirthlin, "Joseph Smith's Boyhood Operation: An 1813 Surgical Success," *BYU Studies* 21.2 (spring 1981): 131–54; and *Ensign,* March 1978, 59–60.

CHAPTER 2: APPEARANCE AND PERSONALITY

1. *St. Louis Weekly Gazette,* June 1844, cited in John Henry Evans, *Joseph Smith: An American Prophet* (New York: Macmillan, 1946), 178–79.
2. James Palmer, "Reminiscences," 69–70, LDS Church Archives.
3. See, for example, Parley P. Pratt, *Autobiography of Parley P. Pratt,* rev. ed. (Salt Lake City: Deseret Book, 2000), 45.
4. *Young Woman's Journal,* vol. 16, no. 12, December 1905, 549.
5. *St. Louis Weekly Gazette,* June 1844.
6. *CHC,* 2:346.
7. *St. Louis Weekly Gazette,* June 1844.
8. *Young Woman's Journal,* vol. 16, no. 12, December 1905, 549.
9. *CHC,* 2:346.
10. *St. Louis Weekly Gazette,* June 1844.
11. Pratt, *Autobiography,* 45.
12. Palmer, "Reminiscences," 69–70.
13. *CHC,* 2:350.
14. Zina D. Young, autobiography, 4, LDS Church Archives.
15. *Overland Monthly,* vol. 16, no. 96, December 1890, 621.
16. John D. Lee, *Mormonism Unveiled* (St. Louis: N. D. Thompson and Co., 1881), 76.
17. See, for instance, Palmer, "Reminiscences," 69–70.

18. See Pratt, *Autobiography*, 45.
19. *CHC*, 2:346.
20. Palmer, "Reminiscences," 69–70.
21. Zina D. Young, autobiography, 4.
22. See Lee, *Mormonism Unveiled*, 76.
23. Palmer, "Reminiscences," 69–70.
24. Lee, *Mormonism Unveiled*, 76.
25. See *St. Louis Weekly Gazette,* June 1844.
26. Ibid.
27. *Improvement Era,* vol. 32, no. 7, May 1929, 541.
28. See E. Dale LeBaron, *Benjamin Franklin Johnson: Friend to the Prophets* (Provo, UT: Grandin Book, 1997), 232.
29. Palmer, "Reminiscences," 69–70.
30. See *Utah Genealogical and Historical Magazine* 6 (July 1915): 147–48.
31. See *Overland Monthly,* vol. 16, no. 96, December 1890, 621.
32. See Brian H. Stuy, ed., *Collected Discourses* (Burbank, CA; Woodland Hills, UT: B. H. S. Publishing, 1987–92), 5:34.
33. See Lee, *Mormonism Unveiled,* 76.
34. See Stuy, ed., *Collected Discourses,* 5:34.
35. Thomas Ford, *A History of Illinois* (Chicago: S. C. Griggs and Co., 1854), 354–55.
36. *St. Louis Weekly Gazette,* June 1844.
37. See *Millennial Star,* vol. 27, no. 30, 29 July 1865, 473; Palmer, "Reminiscences," 341; *Women's Exponent,* vol. 11, no. 8, 15 September 1882, 68; and *Juvenile Instructor,* vol. 27, no. 1, 1 January 1892, 24.
38. *CHC,* 2:346.
39. *St. Louis Weekly Gazette,* June 1844.
40. See *BYU Studies* 10.4 (summer 1970): 481.
41. See Susa Young Gates, *Lydia Knight's History* (Salt Lake City: Juvenile Instructor's Office, 1883), 17.
42. Palmer, "Reminiscences," 69–70.
43. *Salt Lake Herald,* 12 January 1895.
44. *New York Herald,* 19 February 1842; the same weight is given in *Salt Lake Herald,* 12 January 1895.
45. See *Juvenile Instructor,* vol. 27, no. 2, 15 January 1892, 66; Amasa Potter, "Reminiscences and Journal of Amasa Potter," LDS Church Archives; George Moore, diary, 106, cited in Donald Q. Cannon, "Reverend George Moore Comments on Nauvoo, the Mormons, and Joseph Smith," *Western Illinois Regional Studies* 5 (spring 1982): 11; and LeBaron, *Benjamin Franklin Johnson,* 232.
46. See Glen F. Harding, "A Record of the Ancestry and Descendants of John Jacob Zundel, Known as Jacob Zundel," 90, LDS Family History Library, Salt Lake City, UT; *Young Woman's Journal,* vol. 16, no. 12, December 1905, 549–50.
47. *BYU Studies* 40.2 (2001): 171.
48. *Young Woman's Journal,* vol. 17, no. 12, December 1905, 556.
49. Pratt, *Autobiography,* 45.
50. *Juvenile Instructor,* vol. 27, no. 10, 15 May 1892, 302.
51. *HC,* 5:411.
52. *Young Woman's Journal,* vol. 17, no. 12, December 1906, 544.
53. Ford, *A History of Illinois,* 354–55.
54. *Juvenile Instructor,* vol. 27, no. 1, 15 January 1892, 56–57.
55. See LeBaron, *Benjamin Franklin Johnson,* 221.
56. Jacob Jones, testimony, LDS Church Archives.
57. Edwin Rushton, statement, LDS Church Archives.
58. See *BYU Studies* 18.2 (winter 1978): 144–45.
59. Joseph Smith, journal, 18 March 1843, LDS Church Archives, cited in *BYU Studies* 21.2 (spring 1981): 184.
60. Emily Partridge Young, "Statement Written 27 June 1897," LDS Church Archives.
61. See *Juvenile Instructor,* vol. 27, no. 4, 15 February 1892, 127–28.
62. *PWJS,* 399.
63. *JD,* 3:66–67.
64. *WJS,* 206.
65. William I. Appleby, "Diary and Reminiscence," 30 April 1841, LDS Church Archives.
66. Peter H. Burnett, *An Old California Pioneer* (Oakland, CA: Biobooks, 1946), 40–41.
67. *BYU Studies* 18.3 (spring 1978): 478 (italics in original).
68. Ibid, 17.3 (spring 1977): 343.
69. John M. Bernhisel to Thomas Ford, 14 June 1844, LDS Church Archives.
70. *Lucy's Book,* 344.
71. Brigham Young, remarks at general conference, 8 October 1866, LDS Church Archives.
72. *Juvenile Instructor,* vol. 27, no. 1, 1 January 1892, 24.
73. Stuy, ed., *Collected Discourses,* 5:34.
74. *Juvenile Instructor,* vol. 27, no. 6, 15 March 1892, 173–74.
75. William H. Walker, *The Life Incidents and Travels of Elder William Holmes Walker, and His Association with Joseph Smith, the Prophet* (Elizabeth Jane Walker Piepgrass, 1943), 10.
76. See *Young Woman's Journal,* vol. 2, September 1891, 574; and Jared Carter, journal, typescript, 3 June 1831, LDS Church Archives.
77. Burnett, *An Old California Pioneer,* 40.
78. *WJS,* 381.
79. *Young Woman's Journal,* vol. 17, no. 12, December 1906, 544.
80. See James J. Monroe, diary, 110, cited in George W. Givens, *In Old Nauvoo: Everyday Life in the City of Joseph* (Salt Lake City: Deseret Book, 1990), 148.
81. *WJS,* 61.
82. *HC,* 6:303.
83. *BYU Studies* 40.2 (2001): 171, 173.
84. *JD,* 5:332.
85. *WJS,* 32.
86. George A. Smith, journal, 1 June 1834, LDS Church Archives.
87. Christopher Crary, *Pioneer and Personal Reminiscences* (Marshalltown, IA: Marshall Printing Co., 1893), 21. One contemporary newspaper report relates that "as a public speaker he was bold, powerful, and convincing," *New York Herald*, 19 February 1842.
88. Pratt, *Autobiography,* 45.
89. *Improvement Era,* February 1937, 84.
90. *Young Woman's Journal,* vol. 16, no. 12, December 1905, 558.

CHAPTER 3: THE PROPHET'S CHARACTER

1. *HC,* 5:181.
2. *Messenger and Advocate,* vol. 1, no. 3, December 1834, 40.
3. *HC,* 5:516.
4. See ibid., 6:412.
5. LaFayette C. Lee, notebook, LDS Church Archives.
6. *JD,* 7:100.
7. William H. Walker, *The Life Incidents and Travels of Elder William Holmes Walker, and His Association with Joseph Smith, the Prophet* (Elizabeth Jane Walker Piepgrass, 1943), 8–9.
8. Lee, notebook.
9. See *JD,* 10:165; Lula Campbell, "Wandering Home: Stories and Memories of Ira Stearns Hatch, Meltiar Hatch, and John Henry Hatch, and Their Wives and Children," 3–5, LDS Family History Library, Salt Lake City, UT.
10. *Young Woman's Journal,* vol. 17, no. 12, December 1906, 540.
11. Lee, notebook.
12. *Juvenile Instructor,* vol. 27, no. 5, 1 March 1892, 151.
13. Wandle Mace, autobiography, typescript, 79–80, L. Tom Perry Special Collections.
14. *Messenger and Advocate,* vol. 2, no. 3, December 1835, 240.
15. *Warsaw Signal,* 1 June 1841.
16. Brian H. Stuy, ed., *Collected Discourses* (Burbank, CA; Woodland Hills, UT: B. H. S. Publishing, 1987–92), 5:28; see also *HC,* 5:316.
17. Conference Report, October 1897, 64; *Elders' Journal,* vol. 1, no. 4, August 1838, 51.
18. Lee, notebook.
19. *Young Woman's Journal,* vol. 17, no. 12, December 1906, 539.
20. See *HC,* 1:105.

21. *Deseret News,* 16 August 1878, 2.
22. *Relief Society Magazine,* vol. 31, March 1944, 136.
23. *Young Woman's Journal,* vol. 16, no. 12, December 1905, 550.
24. Mary Fielding to Mercy Thompson, July 1837, LDS Church Archives.
25. *Millennial Star,* vol. 48, no. 25, 21 June 1886, 389.
26. Edward W. Tullidge, *The Women of Mormondom* (New York: Tullidge and Crandall, 1877), 66.
27. Walker, *Life Incidents,* 8.
28. *JD,* 7:176.
29. *PWJS,* 264.
30. Ibid., 128, 145, 308, 82.

CHAPTER 4: ENJOYMENTS AND TRIALS

1. *Times and Seasons,* vol. 6, no. 17, 15 November 1845, 1028.
2. *PWJS,* 490.
3. See ibid., 341.
4. See ibid., 36.
5. See *HC,* 2:405.
6. See ibid., 5:418.
7. See "History of George A. Smith," 24 May 1833, LDS Church Archives.
8. See *HC,* 6:133; 5:369; 6:2–3; 5:265; and *Juvenile Instructor,* vol. 27, no. 7, 1 April 1892, 202.
9. John M. Bernhisel to Thomas Ford, 14 June 1844, Bernhisel Collection, LDS Church Archives.
10. E. Dale LeBaron, *Benjamin Franklin Johnson: Friend to the Prophets* (Provo, UT: Grandin Book, 1997), 220.
11. "John Riggs Murdock," in Orson F. Whitney, *History of Utah* (Salt Lake City: George Q. Cannon and Sons, 1904), 4:190–91.
12. See Callie O. Morley, "History of William and Myra Mayall Henrie, Pioneers of 1847," 4–5, LDS Church Archives; Edwin F. Parry, *Stories about Joseph Smith, the Prophet* (Salt Lake City: Deseret News Press, 1934), 18; and *Young Woman's Journal,* vol. 17, no. 12, December 1906, 537–38.
13. See Aroet L. Hale, "First Book or Journal of the Life and Travels of Aroet L. Hale," 24, LDS Church Archives.
14. Ibid.
15. See *HC,* 4:191.
16. Jacob Jones, testimony, LDS Church Archives.
17. See John D. Lee, *Mormonism Unveiled* (St. Louis: N. D. Thompson and Co., 1881), 76. This same source states, "Very few of the Saints had the strength needed to throw the Prophet in a fair tussle." Yet, there are a handful of reports indicating that he was sometimes outwrestled.
18. See Thelma Miller Higbee, "Stories of the Association of the William Henrie Family with the Prophet Joseph Smith as Told to Me by My Aunt Mary Henrie Cooper," 1–2, LDS Church Archives.
19. Howard Coray, autobiography, 10, L. Tom Perry Special Collections.
20. *HC,* 5:279–80, 282.
21. See ibid., 4:601.
22. See "Biographical Sketch of the Life of Peter Wilson Conover," LDS Church Archives; and Edward Stevenson, autobiography, typescript, LDS Church Archives.
23. *Juvenile Instructor,* vol. 27, no. 10, 15 May 1892, 302–3.
24. *HC,* 6:361–62.
25. See LeBaron, *Benjamin Franklin Johnson,* 220.
26. See *Times and Seasons,* vol. 4, no. 6, 1 February 1843, 82–85.
27. Jacob Jones, testimony.
28. LeBaron, *Benjamin Franklin Johnson,* 220.
29. *Woman's Exponent,* vol. 39, no. 2, August 1910, 14.
30. *PWJS,* 449. Note that in this particular reference Joseph attributes his writing imperfections to trembling nerves "from long confinement" in Liberty Jail.
31. Ibid., 287.
32. Ibid., 325 (italics in original).
33. Peter H. Burnett, *An Old California Pioneer* (Oakland, CA: Biobooks, 1946), 40.
34. *JD,* 2:220.

35. Ibid., 10:67.
36. See *Lucy's Book,* 303–9.
37. See *HC,* 2:114; and *Lucy's Book,* 576–78.
38. See *HC,* 1:271.
39. Mary Fielding to Mercy Thompson, July 1837, LDS Church Archives.
40. Brigham Young, journal, 22 July 1839, cited in *New Era,* March 1971, 17.
41. See Philo Dibble, diary, cited in *Ensign,* July 1975, 66.
42. See *Ensign,* January 1979, 28. The Prophet's feelings about debt are recorded in his journal. On 23 September 1835 he wrote: "My heart is full of desire today, to be blessed of the God of Abraham with prosperity, until I will be able to pay all my debts, for it is the delight of my soul to be honest. O Lord, that Thou knowest right well! Help me and I will give to the poor." *PWJS,* 83.
43. *Ensign,* October 1975, 51.
44. See *HC,* 4:437–38.
45. *JD,* 3:112.
46. Ibid., 2:257.
47. See *Times and Seasons,* vol. 3, no. 12, 15 April 1842, 753.
48. See *Kansas City Times,* 11 April 1895.
49. *HC,* 1:88.
50. *Lucy's Book,* 386; *Kansas City Times,* 11 April 1895.
51. *HC,* 1:91.
52. See ibid., 1:261–65.
53. See ibid., 5:442–43; and Wandle Mace, autobiography, typescript, 85–89, L. Tom Perry Special Collections.
54. *PWJS,* 400.
55. Ibid., 427.

CHAPTER 5: A DISCIPLE IN THOUGHT, WORD, AND DEED

1. *PWJS,* 509.
2. Ibid., 252.
3. Ibid., 27.
4. Ibid., 405–6.
5. Ibid., 564.
6. Ibid., 264–65.
7. *HC,* 3:201.
8. See also *Times and Seasons,* vol. 3, no. 9, 1 March 1842, 709–10.
9. *HC,* 3:30.
10. *JD,* 9:365.
11. *HC,* 1:468.
12. Ibid., 4:230.
13. Ibid., 5:141.
14. Ibid., 6:427.
15. *BYU Studies* 18.3 (spring 1978): 479. Joseph Smith stated in the Church's newspaper that a Latter-day Saint is "to feed the hungry, to clothe the naked, to provide for the widow, to dry up the tear of the orphan, to comfort the afflicted, whether in this Church, or in any other, or in no church at all, wherever he finds them . . . [and] to do good unto all men." *Times and Seasons,* vol. 3, no. 10, 15 March 1842, 732.
16. *Juvenile Instructor,* vol. 27, no. 5, 1 March 1892, 152–53.
17. Edwin F. Parry, *Stories about Joseph Smith the Prophet* (Salt Lake City: Deseret News Press, 1934), 100–102.
18. *Millennial Star,* vol. 27, no. 7, 18 February 1865, 103.
19. *Young Woman's Journal,* vol. 16, no. 12, December 1905, 551–52.
20. See *HC,* 2:288–90; 5:290, 298.
21. John Harper, "Record Made by John Harper," LDS Church Archives.
22. Wandle Mace, autobiography, typescript, 41–42, L. Tom Perry Special Collections.
23. *Young Woman's Journal,* vol. 17, no. 12, December 1906, 538.
24. *WJS,* 370.
25. Callie O. Morley, "History of William and Myra Mayall Henrie, Pioneers of 1847," 4–5, LDS Church Archives.

CHAPTER 6: RESTORING GOD'S KINGDOM

1. *JD,* 7:289–90.
2. *BYU Studies* 23.1 (winter 1983): 10, 12. On pages 12 and 13 of this

same source Phelps refers to the Prophet as "the Prince of light" (possibly in connection with his ability to illuminate difficult gospel subjects with his insightful commentary). "President [Lorenzo] Snow reported that on one occasion Joseph Smith was . . . asked who he was. The Prophet smiled kindly upon his interlocutor and replied, 'Noah came before the flood; I have come before the fire.'" Abraham H. Cannon, diary, 1 January 1892, LDS Church Archives.

3. Orson F. Whitney, *Life of Heber C. Kimball*, 2nd ed. (Salt Lake City: Bookcraft, 1945), 322.

4. George Q. Cannon, *Life of Joseph Smith the Prophet* (Salt Lake City: Deseret News Press, 1907), 3.

5. *HC*, 2:443.

6. *WJS*, 155.

7. *HC*, 4:536.

8. Ibid., 5:516.

9. See ibid., 6:365.

10. Ibid., 4:492.

11. E. Dale LeBaron, *Benjamin Franklin Johnson: Friend to the Prophets* (Provo, UT: Grandin Book, 1997), 220.

12. For information regarding many of the Prophet's visions, see Alexander L. Baugh, "Parting the Veil: The Visions of Joseph Smith," *BYU Studies* 38.1 (1999): 23–69. An extended, but probably incomplete, list of Joseph Smith's heavenly visitors can be found in Matthew B. Brown, *All Things Restored: Confirming the Authenticity of LDS Beliefs* (American Fork, UT: Covenant Communications, 2000), 40. An excellent resource on Joseph Smith's revelations (which includes a list of some that were never published) is Lyndon W. Cook, *The Revelations of the Prophet Joseph Smith* (Salt Lake City: Deseret Book, 1985).

13. Both James Palmer and Edward Stevenson heard Joseph Smith identify the angel Moroni as the heavenly messenger described in Revelation 14:6. See James Palmer, "Reminiscences," 72–77, LDS Church Archives; and Edward Stevenson, "The Home of My Boyhood," *Juvenile Instructor*, vol. 29, no. 14, 15 July 1894, 445.

14. Scott H. Faulring, "The Book of Mormon: A Blueprint for Organizing the Church," *Journal of Book of Mormon Studies* 7.1 (1998): 60–69, 71; John A. Tvedtnes, "The Role of the Book of Mormon in the Restoration of the Church," transcript (Provo, UT: FARMS, 1997); Robert J. Woodford, "The Articles and Covenants of the Church of Christ and the Book of Mormon," in *Doctrines for Exaltation* (Salt Lake City: Deseret Book, 1989), 262–73.

15. See Matthew B. Brown, *The Gate of Heaven: Insights on the Doctrines and Symbols of the Temple* (American Fork, UT: Covenant Communications, 1999), 57–247.

16. See Matthew B. Brown, *The Plan of Salvation: Doctrinal Notes and Commentary* (American Fork, UT: Covenant Communications, 2002), 149–57.

17. See *HC*, 1:238.

18. See *Ensign*, January 1997, 52.

19. See ibid., January 1993, 12.

20. See *WJS*, 382.

21. *HC*, 6:305.

22. *WJS*, 60.

23. See Daniel H. Ludlow, ed., *Encyclopedia of Mormonism* (New York: Macmillan, 1992), 1:326–27; and *BYU Studies* 20.2 (winter 1980): 163–92.

24. See *BYU Studies* 16.2 (winter 1976): 202; 20.2 (winter 1980): 186–88; 20.3 (spring 1980): 263, 268; and 23.1 (winter 1983): 11.

25. Brian H. Stuy, ed., *Collected Discourses* (Burbank, CA; Woodland Hills, UT: B. H. S. Publishing, 1991), 4:111.

CHAPTER 7: PUBLIC PROFESSIONS

1. In a letter dated 8 September 1842 Joseph Smith referred to himself as "a patriot and lover of my country." *HC*, 5:159.

2. Dean C. Jessee, "The Kirtland Diary of Wilford Woodruff," *BYU Studies* 12.4 (summer 1972): 390.

3. See *HC*, 1:357–59.

4. Ibid., 1:358.

5. Joseph Smith to Emma Smith, 4 April 1839, LDS Church Archives.

6. Daniel H. Ludlow, ed., *Encyclopedia of Mormonism* (New York: Macmillan, 1992), 3:1269–70.

7. *Times and Seasons*, vol. 2, no. 5, 1 January 1841, 260.

8. See *HC*, 4:293. For further reading see Donald Q. Cannon, "Joseph Smith and the University of Nauvoo," in *Joseph Smith: The Prophet, the Man*, ed. Susan Easton Black and Charles D. Tate Jr. (Provo, UT: BYU Religious Studies Center, 1993), 285–300.

9. See Ludlow, *Encyclopedia of Mormonism*, 3:1348.

10. Pomeroy Tucker, *Origin, Rise, and Progress of Mormonism* (New York: D. Appleton and Co., 1867), 12. Another source includes butter mints among the wares that the Smith family manufactured and sold. See *BYU Studies* 10.3 (spring 1970): 355.

11. *HC*, 4:491.

12. See *BYU Studies* 32.1–2 (1992): 38.

13. *HC*, 4:483. The merchandise was so voluminous that some of it had to be stored in the second story of the building and also in the cellar.

14. *HC*, 4:492.

15. See George W. Givens, *In Old Nauvoo: Everyday Life in the City of Joseph* (Salt Lake City: Deseret Book, 1990), 83–84.

16. *HC*, 4:492.

17. See Givens, *In Old Nauvoo*, 84.

18. Peter Crawley, "A Bibliography of The Church of Jesus Christ of Latter-day Saints in New York, Ohio, and Missouri," *BYU Studies* 12.4 (summer 1972): 518–20.

19. *Times and Seasons*, vol. 1, no. 1, November 1839, 16.

20. See ibid., vol. 3, no. 8, 15 February 1842, 696.

21. See ibid., vol. 3, no. 9, 1 March 1842, 710.

22. See ibid., vol. 4, no. 6, 1 February 1843, 95.

23. See *HC*, 5:489–90.

24. Ibid., 4:309–10.

25. Ibid., 4:355.

26. Ibid., 4:382.

27. Ibid., 5:383–84.

28. Givens, *In Old Nauvoo*, 134.

29. *HC*, 5:56.

30. "Account of the Life of Sarah Burbank, Written at Richfield, Utah, March 13, 1924," Mormon Biography File, LDS Church Archives.

31. Mary Stevenson Clark, autobiography, LDS Church Archives.

32. *HC*, 6:187–88.

33. Ibid.; *Times and Seasons*, vol. 5, no. 11, 1 June 1844, 547.

34. *HC*, 6:187–88.

35. See Joseph Smith, *General Smith's Views of the Powers and Policy of the Government of the United States* (Nauvoo, IL: John Taylor, 1844), 1–12.

36. *HC*, 6:210–11.

37. Ibid., 6:361. For further reading, see Arnold K. Garr, "Joseph Smith: Candidate for President of the United States," in *Regional Studies in Latter-day Saint History: Illinois*, ed. H. Dean Garrett (Provo, UT: Department of Church History and Doctrine, 1995), 151–65; and James B. Allen, "Was Joseph Smith a serious candidate for the presidency of the United States, or was he only attempting to publicize gospel views on public issues?" *Ensign*, September 1973, 21–22.

CHAPTER 8: EVIDENCES OF A DIVINE CALLING

1. *HC*, 6:317.

2. *WJS*, 179.

3. Dennison L. Harris, statement to President Joseph F. Smith, Ephraim, Utah, 15 May 1881, recorded by George F. Gibbs, LDS Church Archives.

4. See *HC*, 2:381.

5. See Matthew B. Brown, *All Things Restored: Confirming the Authenticity of LDS Beliefs* (American Fork, UT: Covenant Communications, 2000), 40.

6. Reuben Miller, journal, 21 October 1848, 14, LDS Church Archives.

7. Oliver Cowdery to Phineas Young, 23 March 1846, cited in Stanley R. Gunn, *Oliver Cowdery: Second Elder and Scribe* (Salt Lake City: Bookcraft, 1962), 161.

8. *Millennial Star*, vol. 48, no. 27, 5 July 1886, 420.

9. Ibid., vol. 26, no. 26, 25 June 1864, 406.

10. William Pilkington to Vern C. Poulter, 28 February 1930, L. Tom Perry Special Collections.

11. *Juvenile Instructor*, vol. 27, no. 10, 15 May 1892, 303–304.

12. Truman O. Angell, journal, typescript, L. Tom Perry Special Collections.

13. Aaron Lindon Cheney, "History of Elam Cheney," copy in private family possession.

14. See "Statement of Zebedee Coltrin," 3 October 1883, Minutes of the Salt Lake School of Prophets, 66–67, LDS Church Archives.

15. Ibid., 56.

16. Edward Stevenson, *Reminiscences of Joseph, the Prophet, and the Coming Forth of the Book of Mormon* (Salt Lake City: Edward Stevenson, 1893), 4.

17. See, for instance, Karl R. Anderson, *Joseph Smith's Kirtland* (Salt Lake City: Deseret Book, 1989), 168–77; Steven C. Harper, "Pentecost Continued: A Contemporary Account of the Kirtland Temple Dedication," *BYU Studies* 42.2 (2003): 5–22.

18. See *HC*, 1:323. Zebedee Coltrin related that he heard the Prophet not only speak but also sing in tongues. See Zebedee Coltrin, journal, 50, LDS Church Archives.

19. Joseph Young Sr., *History of the Organization of the Seventies* (Salt Lake City: Deseret News Steam Printing Establishment, 1878), 10–11.

20. See Wilford Woodruff, *Leaves from My Journal* (Salt Lake City: Juvenile Instructor's Office, 1882), 62–66; Elden J. Watson, ed., *Manuscript History of Brigham Young: 1801–1844* (Salt Lake City: Smith Secretarial Service, 1968), 49; and Robert B. Thompson, ed., *Journal of Heber C. Kimball* (Nauvoo, IL: Robinson and Smith, 1840), 81–82.

21. Benjamin Brown, *Testimonies for the Truth* (Liverpool, England: Samuel W. Richards, 1853), 12.

22. See *HC*, 2:328.

23. Jared Carter, journal, typescript, LDS Church Archives.

24. *Juvenile Instructor*, vol. 27, no. 12, 15 June 1892, 385–86.

25. *Young Woman's Journal*, vol. 17, no. 12, December 1906, 545.

26. *HC*, 2:80.

27. *Juvenile Instructor*, vol. 27, no. 1, 1 January 1892, 23.

28. *WJS*, 367.

29. *HC*, 2:101–5.

30. Sarah Stoddard, diary, April 1844, cited in Robert H. Daines, "The Doctrine of Christ," in *Brigham Young University 2000–2001 Speeches* (Provo, UT: BYU Publications and Graphics, 2001), 43–44.

CHAPTER 9: MARTYRDOM AT CARTHAGE JAIL

1. *The Contributor*, vol. 5, no. 7, April 1884, 251–60. Several other people also testified to the fact that there was a conspiracy to kill the Prophet. See ibid., vol. 8, no. 10, August 1887, 361–62. For further reading on the martyrdom of Joseph Smith, see Dean C. Jessee, "Return to Carthage: Writing the History of Joseph Smith's Martyrdom," *Journal of Mormon History* 8 (1981): 3–19; Reed Blake, "Martyrdom at Carthage," *Ensign*, June 1994, 30–39; Kenneth W. Godfrey, "Remembering the Deaths of Joseph and Hyrum Smith," in *Joseph Smith: The Prophet, the Man*, ed. Susan Easton Black and Charles D. Tate Jr. (Provo, UT: BYU Religious Studies Center, 1993), 301–15.

2. See Daniel H. Ludlow, *Encyclopedia of Mormonism* (New York: Macmillan, 1992), 3:996–97.

3. Nathan Cheney to Charles Beebe, 28–29 June 1844, LDS Church Archives. See also *HC*, 6:432.

4. For more on this issue, see Dallin H. Oaks, "The Suppression of the *Nauvoo Expositor*," *Utah Law Review* 9 (winter 1965): 862–903.

5. *HC*, 7:4.

6. Ibid., 6:540.

7. Ibid., 6:547.

8. Ibid., 6:545.

9. Ibid., 6:549–50.

10. William W. Phelps, "Joseph Smith's Last Dream," LDS Church Archives.

11. Dan Jones, "The Martyrdom of Joseph Smith and His Brother Hyrum!" *BYU Studies* 24.1 (winter 1984): 86.

12. Ibid., 88.

13. Cyrus H. Wheelock to George A. Smith, 29 December 1854, cited in Jessee, "Return to Carthage," 8.

14. See *Times and Seasons*, vol. 5, no. 12, 1 July 1844, 561–64.

15. Stephen Markham to Wilford Woodruff, 20 June 1856, LDS Church Archives.

16. *HC*, 6:600.

17. John Taylor referred to the Carthage Greys militia as being "a company strictly mobocratic; and whom we knew to be our most deadly enemies" (*HC*, 7:100).

18. Dan Jones to Thomas Bullock, 20 January 1855, LDS Church Archives.

19. *Daily Democrat*, 10 May 1885.

20. William M. Daniels, affidavit sworn before Justice of the Peace Aaron Johnson, 4 July 1844, cited in *HC*, 7:162–63.

21. Cyrus H. Wheelock to George A. Smith, 29 December 1854, cited in Jessee, "Return to Carthage," 8–9. Wheelock's revolver originally belonged to John Taylor and was given to Wheelock prior to their going to Carthage (see *HC*, 7:100).

22. Ibid., 7:101.

23. John Taylor, discourse, 27 June 1854, transcript, LDS Church Archives.

24. See *HC*, 7:101.

25. See D&C 135:4–5.

26. *HC*, 7:101–2.

27. This reconstruction of events is taken from *Times and Seasons*, vol. 5, no. 14, 1 August 1844, 598–99; *HC*, 7:101–5; Willard Richards to Brigham Young, 30 June 1844, draft, LDS Church Archives. For information regarding the wounding of the mob members by Joseph Smith, see *Ensign*, June 1994, 39 n. 26.

28. People vs. Aldrich, et. al., Mormon Collection, Chicago Historical Society, Chicago; see Thomas Dixon, testimony, recorded by George D. Watt, LDS Church Archives.

29. William Terrel, statement, 3 January 1902, LDS Church Archives.

30. William M. Daniels, testimony, in transcript of Carthage Court Trial, May 1845, recorded by George D. Watt, LDS Church Archives. The William Daniels account of the martyrdom (and the light) was distorted in an 1845 pamphlet published in Nauvoo, Illinois, by Lyman O. Littlefield. Daniels repudiated the pamphlet's version of events while testifying under oath in May 1845, and therefore its contents should not be accounted as being accurate. However, a report by Mary E. Lightner corroborates Daniels's story about the light. She says that several men from her town of Pontoonsuc, Illinois, went to Carthage after Joseph and Hyrum had been arrested. The day after the martyrdom, about ten men came to her door, stating that "the Smiths were killed and that a great light appeared at their death." Mary Elizabeth Rollins Lightner, journal, 24, Utah State Historical Society, Salt Lake City, UT.

31. See *HC*, 6:626–28.

32. See ibid., 6:628–29.

CONCLUSION

1. *HC*, 6:628.

2. Richard Van Wagoner and Steven C. Walker, "The Joseph/Hyrum Smith Funeral Sermon," *BYU Studies* 23.1 (winter 1983): 3–18.

3. *Times and Seasons*, vol. 5, no. 14, 1 August 1844, 607.

SELECTED BIBLIOGRAPHY

Listed here are some of the sources that have been cited in this book. The reader may find this collection useful as a guide for further study. The Church Archives of The Church of Jesus Christ of Latter-day Saints in Salt Lake City is identified as LDS Church Archives. The L. Tom Perry Special Collections is located in the Harold B. Lee Library at Brigham Young University, Provo, Utah.

BOOKS AND ARTICLES

Allen, James B. "Was Joseph Smith a serious candidate for the presidency of the United States, or was he only attempting to publicize gospel views on public issues?" *Ensign,* September 1973, 21–22.

Alvord, Samuel Morgan. *A Genealogy of the Descendants of Alexander Alvord, an Early Settler of Windsor, Conn., and Northampton, Mass.* Webster, NY: A. D. Andrews, 1908.

Anderson, Karl R. *Joseph Smith's Kirtland.* Salt Lake City: Deseret Book, 1989.

Anderson, Lavina F., ed. *Lucy's Book: A Critical Edition of Lucy Mack Smith's Family Memoir.* Salt Lake City: Signature Books, 2001.

Anderson, Richard L. *Investigating the Book of Mormon Witnesses.* Salt Lake City: Deseret Book, 1981.

Blake, Reed. "Martyrdom at Carthage." *Ensign,* June 1994, 30–39.

Brown, Benjamin. *Testimonies for the Truth.* Liverpool, England: Samuel W. Richards, 1853.

Brown, Matthew B. *The Gate of Heaven: Insights on the Doctrines and Symbols of the Temple.* American Fork, UT: Covenant Communications, 1999.

———. *All Things Restored: Confirming the Authenticity of LDS Beliefs.* American Fork, UT: Covenant Communications, 2000.

———. *The Plan of Salvation: Doctrinal Notes and Commentary.* American Fork, UT: Covenant Communications, 2002.

Burnett, Peter H. *An Old California Pioneer.* Oakland, CA: Biobooks, 1946.

Cannon, Donald Q. "Reverend George Moore Comments on Nauvoo, the Mormons, and Joseph Smith." *Western Illinois Regional Studies* 5 (spring 1982): 5–16.

———. "Joseph Smith and the University of Nauvoo." In *Joseph Smith: The Prophet, the Man,* edited by Susan Easton Black and Charles D. Tate Jr., 285–300. Provo, UT: BYU Religious Studies Center, 1993.

Cannon, George Q. *Life of Joseph Smith the Prophet.* Salt Lake City: Deseret News Press, 1907.

Crary, Christopher. *Pioneer and Personal Reminiscences.* Marshalltown, IA: Marshall Printing Co., 1893.

Crawley, Peter. "A Bibliography of The Church of Jesus Christ of Latter-day Saints in New York, Ohio, and Missouri." *BYU Studies* 12.4 (summer 1972): 465–538.

Ehat, Andrew F., and Lyndon W. Cook, eds. *The Words of Joseph Smith: The Contemporary Accounts of the Nauvoo Discourses of the Prophet Joseph.* Orem, UT: Grandin Book, 1991.

Evans, John Henry. *Joseph Smith: An American Prophet.* New York: Macmillan, 1946.

Faulring, Scott H. "The Book of Mormon: A Blueprint for Organizing the Church." *Journal of Book of Mormon Studies* 7.1 (1998): 60–69, 71.

Garr, Arnold K. "Joseph Smith: Candidate for President of the United States." In *Regional Studies in Latter-day Saint History: Illinois,* edited by H. Dean Garrett, 151–65. Provo, UT: Department of Church History and Doctrine, 1995.

Gates, Susa Young. *Lydia Knight's History.* Salt Lake City: Juvenile Instructor's Office, 1883.

Givens, George W. *In Old Nauvoo: Everyday Life in the City of Joseph.* Salt Lake City: Deseret Book, 1990.

Godfrey, Kenneth W. "Remembering the Deaths of Joseph and Hyrum Smith." In *Joseph Smith: The Prophet, the Man,* edited by Susan Easton Black and Charles D. Tate, 301–15. Provo, UT: BYU Religious Studies Center, 1993.

Gunn, Stanley R. *Oliver Cowdery: Second Elder and Scribe.* Salt Lake City: Bookcraft, 1962.

Harper, Steven C. "Pentecost Continued: A Contemporaneous Account of the Kirtland Temple Dedication." *BYU Studies* 42.2 (2003): 5–22.

Jessee, Dean C. "The Kirtland Diary of Wilford Woodruff." *BYU Studies* 12.4 (summer 1972): 365–99.

———. "Return to Carthage: Writing the History of Joseph Smith's Martyrdom." *Journal of Mormon History* 8 (1981): 3–19.

———, ed. *Personal Writings of Joseph Smith.* Rev. ed. Salt Lake City: Deseret Book; Provo, UT: Brigham Young University Press, 2002.

LeBaron, E. Dale. *Benjamin Franklin Johnson: Friend to the Prophets.* Provo, UT: Grandin Book, 1997.

Lee, John D. *Mormonism Unveiled.* St. Louis: N. D. Thompson and Co., 1881.

Ludlow, Daniel H., ed. *Encyclopedia of Mormonism.* 4 vols. New York: Macmillan, 1992.

Oaks, Dallin H. "The Suppression of the *Nauvoo Expositor.*" *Utah Law Review* 9 (winter 1965): 862–903.

Parry, Edwin F. *Stories about Joseph Smith, the Prophet.* Salt Lake City: Deseret News Press, 1934.

Pratt, Orson. *An Interesting Account of Several Remarkable Visions.* Edinburgh, Scotland: Ballantyne and Hughes, 1840.

Pratt, Parley P. *Autobiography of Parley P. Pratt.* Rev. ed. Salt Lake City: Deseret Book, 2000.

Roberts, Brigham H. *A Comprehensive History of The Church of Jesus Christ of Latter-day Saints.* 6 vols. Salt Lake City: Deseret News Press, 1930.

———, ed. *History of The Church of Jesus Christ of Latter-day Saints.* 4th ed. 7 vols. Salt Lake City: Deseret News Press, 1965.

Smith, Joseph. *General Smith's Views of the Powers and Policy of the Government of the United States.* Nauvoo, IL: John Taylor, 1844.

Stevenson, Edward. *Reminiscences of Joseph, the Prophet, and the Coming Forth of the Book of Mormon.* Salt Lake City: Edward Stevenson, 1893.

Stuy, Brian H., ed. *Collected Discourses.* 5 vols. Burbank, CA; Woodland Hills, UT: B. H. S. Publishing, 1987–92.

Tucker, Pomeroy. *Origin, Rise, and Progress of Mormonism.* New York: D. Appleton and Co., 1867.

Tullidge, Edward W. *The Women of Mormondom.* New York: Tullidge and Crandall, 1877.

Turner, Orsamus. *History of the Pioneer Settlement of Phelps and Gorham's Purchase, and Morris Reserve.* Rochester, NY: William Alling, 1851.

Tvedtnes, John A. "The Role of the Book of Mormon in the Restoration of the Church." Transcript. Provo, UT: FARMS, 1997.

Van Wagoner, Richard, and Steven C. Walker. "The Joseph/Hyrum Smith Funeral Sermon." *BYU Studies* 23.1 (winter 1983): 3–18.

Watt, George D., ed. *Journal of Discourses.* 26 vols. Liverpool, England: Franklin D. Richards and Sons, 1854–86.

Whitney, Orson F. *History of Utah.* 4 vols. Salt Lake City: George Q. Cannon and Sons, 1904.

———. *Life of Heber C. Kimball.* 2nd ed. Salt Lake City: Bookcraft, 1945.

Wirthlin, LeRoy S. "Joseph Smith's Boyhood Operation: An 1813 Surgical Success." *BYU Studies* 21.2 (spring 1981): 131–54.

Woodford, Robert J. "The Articles and Covenants of the Church of Christ and the Book of Mormon." In *Doctrines for Exaltation,* 262–73. Salt Lake City: Deseret Book, 1989.

Woodruff, Wilford. *Leaves from My Journal.* Salt Lake City: Juvenile Instructor's Office, 1882.

Young, Joseph, Sr. *History of the Organization of the Seventies.* Salt Lake City: Deseret News Steam Printing Establishment, 1878.

UNPUBLISHED ARCHIVAL MANUSCRIPTS

"Account of the Life of Sarah Burbank, Written at Richfield, Utah, March 13, 1924." Mormon Biography File. LDS Church Archives.

Angell, Truman O. Journal, typescript. L. Tom Perry Special Collections.

Appleby, William I. "Diary and Reminiscence." LDS Church Archives.

Bernhisel, John M., to Thomas Ford, 14 June 1844. LDS Church Archives.

"Biographical Sketch of the Life of Peter Wilson Conover." LDS Church Archives.

Cannon, Abraham H. Diary. LDS Church Archives.

Carter, Jared. Journal, typescript. LDS Church Archives.

Cheney, Nathan, to Charles Beebe, 28–29 June 1844. LDS Church Archives.

Clark, Mary Stevenson. Autobiography. LDS Church Archives.

Conference in Nauvoo, Illinois, 8 October 1845. General Minutes Collection. LDS Church Archives.

Coray, Howard. Autobiography. L. Tom Perry Special Collections.

Daniels, William M. Affidavit sworn before Justice of the Peace Aaron Johnson, 4 July 1844.

Fielding, Mary, to Mercy Thompson, July 1837. LDS Church Archives.

Hale, Aroet L. "First Book or Journal of the Life and Travels of Aroet L. Hale." LDS Church Archives.

Harding, Glen F. "A Record of the Ancestry and Descendants of John Jacob Zundel, Known as Jacob Zundel." LDS Family History Library, Salt Lake City.

Harper, John. "Record Made by John Harper." LDS Church Archives.

Harris, Dennison L. Statement to President Joseph F. Smith, Ephraim, Utah, 15 May 1881, recorded by George F. Gibbs. LDS Church Archives.

Higbee, Thelma Miller. "Stories of the Association of the William Henrie Family with the Prophet Joseph Smith as Told to Me by My Aunt Mary Henrie Cooper." LDS Church Archives.

Jones, Jacob. Testimony. LDS Church Archives.

Joseph Smith Jr. patriarchal blessing, given by Joseph Smith Sr., 9 December 1834, Kirtland, Ohio. Patriarchal Blessing Book #1. LDS Church Archives.

Lee, LaFayette C. Notebook. LDS Church Archives.

Lightner, Mary Elizabeth Rollins. Journal. Utah State Historical Society, Salt Lake City.

Mace, Wandle. Autobiography, typescript. L. Tom Perry Special Collections.

Miller, Reuben. Journal. LDS Church Archives.

Morley, Callie O. "History of William and Myra Mayall Henrie, Pioneers of 1847." LDS Church Archives.

Palmer, James. "Reminiscences." LDS Church Archives.

Phelps, William W. "Joseph Smith's Last Dream." LDS Church Archives.

Pilkington, William, to Vern C. Poulter, 28 February 1930. L. Tom Perry Special Collections.

Potter, Amasa. "Reminiscences and Journal of Amasa Potter." LDS Church Archives.

Recollection of Mrs. Palmer. In "Stories from the Notebook of Martha Cox, Grandmother of Fern Cox Anderson." LDS Church Archives.

Richards, Willard, to Brigham Young, 30 June 1844, draft. LDS Church Archives.

Rushton, Edwin. Statement. LDS Church Archives.

Smith, George A. Journal. LDS Church Archives.

Smith, Joseph, to Emma Smith, 4 April 1839. LDS Church Archives.

Stevenson, Edward. Autobiography, typescript. LDS Church Archives.

PERIODICALS

Contributor
Daily Democrat
Deseret News
Elders' Journal
Improvement Era
Juvenile Instructor
Kansas City Times
Messenger and Advocate
Millennial Star
New York Herald
Overland Monthly
Relief Society Magazine
Salt Lake Herald
St. Louis Weekly Gazette
Times and Seasons
Utah Genealogical and Historical Magazine
Women's Exponent
Young Woman's Journal

PHOTOGRAPHS & ARTWORK

Page 54: 1835 LDS hymnal, song #26. Photograph © Val W. Brinkerhoff. Shown courtesy of the Daughters of the Utah Pioneers Museum, Salt Lake City, Utah.

Page 56: Manti Temple altar. Photograph © Val W. Brinkerhoff. Shown courtesy of the Museum of Church History and Art, Salt Lake City, Utah.

Page 57: Detail of a handclasp from a headstone in the Old Nauvoo Cemetery. Photograph © Val W. Brinkerhoff.

Page 57: Crown and initials on cane. Photograph © Val W. Brinkerhoff. Shown courtesy of the Museum of Church History and Art, Salt Lake City, Utah.

CHAPTER 7: PUBLIC PROFESSIONS

Page 58–59: Book collection. Photograph by Val W. Brinkerhoff. Copyright © 2004 Community of Christ, used by permission.

Page 60: Plat of the City of Zion. Photograph © Val W. Brinkerhoff. Shown courtesy of the Museum of Church History and Art, Salt Lake City, Utah.

Page 63: Red Brick Store interior. Photograph by Val W. Brinkerhoff. Copyright © 2004 Community of Christ, used by permission.

Page 64: Nauvoo printing press. Photograph © Val W. Brinkerhoff.

Page 64: Nauvoo printing office. Photograph © Val W. Brinkerhoff.

Page 66: *Lieutenant General Joseph Smith: Mormon Prophet* by Sutcliffe Maudsley. © by Intellectual Reserve, Inc. Courtesy of the Museum of Church History and Art, Salt Lake City, Utah.

Page 67: Sword, scabbard, and sash. Photograph by Val W. Brinkerhoff. Copyright © 2004 Community of Christ, used by permission. Shown courtesy of the estate of Alexander Hale Smith.

Page 68: Mansion House office. Photograph by Val W. Brinkerhoff. Copyright © 2004 Community of Christ, used by permission.

Page 69: *Ben Campbell,* upper Mississippi River steamboat. Daguerreotype Collection (no. 1200), prints and photographs division, Library of Congress, Washington, D.C.

CHAPTER 8: EVIDENCES OF A DIVINE CALLING

Page 71: Kirtland Temple. Photograph © Val W. Brinkerhoff.

Page 72–73: *Jesus Christ Visits the Kirtland Temple* by Walter Rane. © by Intellectual Reserve, Inc. Courtesy of the Museum of Church History and Art, Salt Lake City, Utah.

Page 73: Kirtland Temple pulpits. Photograph by Val W. Brinkerhoff. Copyright © 2004 Community of Christ, used by permission.

Page 74: Anthon Transcript. Photograph by Val W. Brinkerhoff. Copyright © 2004 Community of Christ, used by permission.

Page 76–77: School of the Prophets room. Photograph © Val W. Brinkerhoff. Shown courtesy of the Newel K. Whitney Store, operated by The Church of Jesus Christ of Latter-day Saints in Kirtland, Ohio.

Page 77: Newel K. Whitney store exterior. Photograph © Val W. Brinkerhoff.

Page 80: Dark clouds on the Mississippi River. Photograph © Val W. Brinkerhoff.

Page 82: Shotgun above mantel. Photograph © Val W. Brinkerhoff.

Page 82: Homestead well. Photograph © Val W. Brinkerhoff.

CHAPTER 9: MARTYRDOM AT CARTHAGE JAIL

Page 84–85: *Martyrdom at Carthage Jail* by Gary E. Smith. © by Intellectual Reserve, Inc. Courtesy of the Museum of Church History and Art, Salt Lake City, Utah.

Page 87: Dungeon in Carthage Jail. Photograph © Val W. Brinkerhoff. Shown courtesy of the Carthage Jail Visitor's Center in Carthage, Illinois.

Page 88: *Exterior of Carthage Jail* by C. C. A. Christensen. Courtesy of Brigham Young University Museum of Art. All rights reserved. (Image cropped in book, see complete image here.)

Page 89: Powder horn. Photograph © Val W. Brinkerhoff. Shown courtesy of the Museum of Church History and Art, Salt Lake City, Utah.

Page 90–91: Joseph Smith's revolver on Carthage Jail floor. Composite photograph © Val W. Brinkerhoff. Shown courtesy of the Museum of Church History and Art, Salt Lake City, Utah, and the Carthage Jail Visitor's Center in Carthage, Illinois.

Page 91: Bullet hole in Carthage Jail door panel. Photograph © Val W. Brinkerhoff. Shown courtesy of the Carthage Jail Visitor's Center in Carthage, Illinois.

Page 93: View of the water well from the upstairs window of Carthage Jail. Photograph © Val W. Brinkerhoff.

Page 93: Water well outside Carthage Jail. Photograph © Val W. Brinkerhoff.

Page 94: Casts from the death masks of Joseph and Hyrum Smith. Photograph © Val W. Brinkerhoff. Shown courtesy of the Museum of Church History and Art, Salt Lake City, Utah.

CONCLUSION

Page 97: Portrait by Danquart A. Weggeland. Photograph © Val W. Brinkerhoff. Shown courtesy of the Museum of Church History and Art, Salt Lake City, Utah.

ENDSHEETS

Front:

Joseph Smith's dressing case. Photograph by Val W. Brinkerhoff. Copyright © 2004 Community of Christ, used by permission. Shown courtesy of the Lynn Smith Family.

Printer's manuscript pages. Photograph by Val W. Brinkerhoff. Copyright © 2004 Community of Christ, used by permission.

Joseph Smith's Nauvoo Legion shoulder epaulet. Photograph © Val W. Brinkerhoff. Copyright © 2004 Community of Christ, used by permission. Shown courtesy of the estate of Alexander Hale Smith.

Original Kirtland Temple pulpits © 2004 Community of Christ, used by permission.

Razor belonging to Joseph Smith. Photograph © Val W. Brinkerhoff. Shown courtesy of the Daughters of the Utah Pioneers Museum, Salt Lake City, Utah.

Joseph Smith's gravestone (located at the southeast corner of the homestead in Nauvoo, Illinois) © Val W. Brinkerhoff.

Back:

Liberty Jail door. Photograph by Val W. Brinkerhoff. Copyright © 2004 Community of Christ, used by permission.

Liberty Jail key. Photograph by Val W. Brinkerhoff. Copyright © 2004 Community of Christ, used by permission.

Arch detail from Kirtland Temple. Photograph by Val W. Brinkerhoff. Copyright © 2004 Community of Christ, used by permission.

Detail from Nauvoo Temple exterior. Photograph © Val W. Brinkerhoff.